A BIBLICAL
COMMENTARY ON
JAMES

WISDOM IN ACTION!

BRUCE GUCKELBERG, PH.D.

WESTBOW°
PRESS
A DIVISION OF THOMAS NELSON
& ZONDERVAN

WestBow Press books may be ordered through booksellers or by contacting:

WestBow Press
A Division of Thomas Nelson & Zondervan
1663 Liberty Drive
Bloomington, IN 47403
www.westbowpress.com
1 (866) 928-1240

ISBN: 978-1-4908-7733-4 (sc)
ISBN: 978-1-4908-7734-1 (hc)
ISBN: 978-1-4908-7732-7 (e)

Library of Congress Control Number: 2015906209

Print information available on the last page.

WestBow Press rev. date: 05/19/2015

To my loving wife

Carol

CONTENTS

FOREWORD

Written "in the trenches" by a seasoned pastor who both knows his Greek New Testament and also directed his own business before responding to the call of God to teach and preach the Gospel, this commentary will stand out from others on the shelf: it reflects James' own practical and applicable emphases. While familiar with "issues" that may characterize other standard commentaries, Guckelberg deliberately chooses to cut to the quick, passing rapidly through secondary matters, in order to bring to the fore what is salient in each passage. Those who preach every Sunday, as does the author, will appreciate this helpful tool.

Gene R. Smillie, Ph.D.
Trinity International University
Deerfield, Illinois

Author's Preface

James is my favorite book of the Bible because of its practical nature. The topics he covers are ones that the modern reader faces in his everyday life, and are easy to identify with. Whether one is a new believer or a seasoned veteran of the Christian faith, studying James will pay high spiritual dividends. Having preached through the book of James many times, I've found it to be of enormous value to those who want to grow deeper in their walk with the Lord. Its greatest value is for practical Christian living.

Commentaries are flooding the market in record numbers. Never before in my lifetime have I seen so many new commentaries being introduced to the Christian community. When someone writes a commentary on a book of the Bible, there are certain objectives the author has in mind. My objectives in writing this commentary were to write in such a way that there is depth, exegetical accuracy, with ease of readability. I chose not to spend vast amounts of time and space getting bogged down with secondary issues, so I get right to the heart of the text and develop the meaning set forth by James.

I also chose to dispense with endless miles of footnotes, which most people don't ready anyway, and make the commentary more readable. My objective was to get to the heart of the issues James presents for us in a way that is understandable and relevant for the modern reader.

I introduce Greek words when appropriate to enhance the meaning of the text. All passages of Scripture in the commentary are identified by being placed in quotations, and are from the New International Version, unless otherwise stated.

After doing an exegesis of the text I have a section called insights and application, where I offer ideas and stories to illustrate some of the points. Since James is a practical book of the Bible, I wrote this commentary with a view to making it easy to apply for the reader. I believe the greatest task of the writer, Bible teacher, or preacher on Sunday morning is to make the word of God intersect with people's everyday lives.

This commentary will be helpful to the pastor, Sunday school teacher, small group leader, and any disciple of Christ who desires to go deeper in his understanding of this great book of the Bible.

I want to thank my friend Gene Smillie for proofreading the book, and offering his suggestions and insights that he's gained over many years of study, pastoral ministry, missionary work, and teaching at Trinity International University.

I hope this commentary will be a blessing to those who read it.

Bruce Guckelberg

INTRODUCTION

The Author

James is clearly identified as the author of this letter. However, this poses a problem because there are five different James mentioned in the New Testament. The traditional view of authorship is that James—the brother of the Lord Jesus—wrote this letter, which is the view taken in this commentary. A brief sketch of the different James mentioned in Scripture is worthy of attention.

James, the son of Judas, is mentioned in the list of the original 12 disciples that Jesus designated as apostles (Luke 6:16). There were two people among the original 12 that bore the name Judas, so Luke makes a distinction between them identifying one as Judas, who had a son named James. The other is Judas Iscariot, who became a traitor.

The second James is the son of Zebedee, and the brother of John. James and John were known as the "Sons of Thunder", which gives you an idea of what type of people they were—highly explosive. James, John, and Peter were in the inner circle with Jesus, being the unique witnesses to some of the miracles he performed, such as the transfiguration, and Jesus

1

invited them to pray with him in the garden of Gethsemane. James was the first of the original twelve disciples to be put to death around AD 44, which lessens the likelihood that he would be the author of the epistle we are examining. The following passages contain references to James: Matt 4:21, 10:2, 17:1, Mark 1:19, 29, 3:17, 5:37, 9:2. 10:35, 41, 13:3, 14:33, Luke 5:10, 6:14, 8:51, 9:28, 54, Acts 1:13, 12:2.

The third James to consider is James, son of Alphaeus (Matt 10:3, Mark 3:18, Luke 6:15, Acts 1:13), in distinction from James—the brother of John—in the list of the original 12. Little else is known of him, so he would be an unlikely candidate for the author of this letter.

The fourth James is "James the Less" or "little James", who is also the son of Mary (Matt 27:56, Mark 15:40, 16:1, Luke 24:10). This Mary was a witness at Jesus' burial and resurrection. There is debate among scholars as to whether James—the son of Alphaeus—and "James the less" are one and the same person.

Finally, James the son of Joseph and Mary, and half-brother of Jesus, is thought by most scholars to be the author of this letter. He didn't believe that Jesus was the Messiah during his ministry (John 7:5) however, after Jesus rose from the dead he made a special appearance to James, (1 Cor 15:7) which most scholars believe was his brother. That would have been an interesting conversation to witness! One can only imagine what Jesus said to James, and how James felt when he discovered that his big brother really was the Messiah. That was a shock and awe moment for James, no doubt! After James became a believer he was recognized as a key leader in the early church in Jerusalem. He was known for his piety, his fervent prayer life, was highly respected in the Jewish Christian community, and was martyred around AD 62.

Historical Setting

This letter was most likely written in Jerusalem, which is where James lived. The historian Josephus notes that James was condemned to death by the Sanhedrin in AD 62, at which time he suffered a martyr's death. Thus, the letter had to be written prior to that time. A likely date of the letter is between AD 47-49.

With the stoning of Stephen (AD 35), persecution broke out causing many to leave Jerusalem. Saul of Tarsus was one of the instigators of the persecution, but was converted on the road to Damascus (AD 35). There is no mention of the Jewish/Gentile controversy of the fifties and sixties in James' letter. The Jerusalem council was convened to discuss this issue (Acts 15) around AD 50. The letter has no mention of Paul or allusions to his writings, which seems to indicate that this letter was written before Paul's rise to prominence in the church. James doesn't discuss false teachings, which rose to the surface later in the life of the First Century church, and occupied a place in the writings of Paul, Peter, Jude, and John.

For these reasons, the most probable date for James' letter is after the mass persecution, which broke out in AD 35, and before the Jerusalem council in AD 50. Therefore, the position taken in this commentary is that the letter was written somewhere between AD 47-49.

Purpose of Writing

Being forced to leave your hometown and live as refugees would result in many hardships and difficulties. Jesus had told his disciples that they would be witnesses in Judea and Samaria (Acts 1:8), and with the persecution that broke out (Acts 8:1) the disciples scattered to different locations outside of their homeland, and preached the gospel wherever they went.

The persecution turned into a divine church planting program, which points to the hand of God directing the expansion of his church. The gospel had to spread, so through the agency of this persecution God's people entered crisis mode, but told people the Jesus story wherever they went. Thus, new churches were planted, and many people came to believe in the Lord Jesus Christ.

One can only imagine the hardships to be faced by being uprooted and having to rebuild your life from scratch. The trials that would result from such an existence would be overwhelming. Financial problems, persecution, and oppression at the hands of the rich, were some of the problems that had to be overcome by these believers. Additionally, going through so much hardship caused many to question whether or not their commitment to Christ was worth it, so many were tempted to give up, abandoning their walk with the Lord Jesus!

James wrote to these hurting people who were living in crisis mode, to provide them with encouragement, support, and motivation to continue on in the Christian life. He uses more imperatives (commands) than any other New Testament book of the Bible. His concern in writing is practical Christian living. It isn't that James has no interest in theological matters, he just touches briefly on theology and focuses on the impact of theology in the lives of believers. Reading through James is drastically different than reading through the theological complexities found in the book of Romans. James is practical, not theoretical in his writing. This is best illustrated in 1:22 where he says: Do not merely listen to the word, and so deceive yourselves. Do what it says.

Literary Style

James is a very creative thinker! He writes with colorful word pictures and provides his readers with numerous illustrations to drive home his points. For example, he mentions the one who prays without faith "is like a wave of the sea, blown and tossed by the wind (1:6)." He compares the lifecycle of sin, to the lifecycle of a human being (1:13-15), the illustration of the man who looks in the mirror (1:23-25), the illustration of the rich man who comes to church and gets special treatment (2:1-5), are just a few examples of the colorful style in which James writes. Reflecting on the illustrations and word pictures James uses helps the reader to grasp his concepts, and brings her to a point of application in her daily experience.

It is difficult to see connections between some sections in this letter, which suggests that it reads more like a homily than a letter. This was written to his congregations that were scattered away from their homeland, and reads more like a sermon than a letter. There is much redundancy in his homily, for he repeatedly brings up the theme of one's communication, poverty, the law, and at times it seems as though James is randomly going back and forth with his ideas. This isn't to say that there is no structure to James' thoughts, and that no logical connections exist between sections of the sermon. It just seems at times like he's jumping around from one thought to another.

Theological Themes

Real Faith

James' dominant concern expressed throughout his letter is that one's profession of faith in Christ must translate into a lifestyle that reflects that profession (2:14-26). James is all about no nonsense Christianity! Real faith has to produce a lifestyle of good works! The one who is truly born-again will possess a vibrant faith in the Lord that will show that reality in the way he lives. In the absence of good works, one would have to question the veracity of a person's claim to be born-again. For James there is no doubt: one who is born-again is one who excels in good works. Faith has to lead to good works, which indicate that true life transformation through Christ has taken place. The absence of good works indicates that faith is dead (2:17)!

Trials

James' audience was living in crisis mode! These people were living under extreme pressure after being forced to leave their hometown, Jerusalem, and rebuild their lives from scratch. Under that kind of pressure some were wondering if becoming a Christian was really worth the sacrifice, and were contemplating walking away from Jesus! James provides much counsel for believers who are going through difficult trials (1:1-8). He helps suffering believers see how God works through trials for their benefit. Often times Christians experience much growth by going through the crucible of tribulation, and James helps us to understand that truth, while offering suggestions about how to have a good attitude during difficult times. As the pastor of these hurting believers, he is trying to encourage them to hang in there through their difficulties, and point them to the reward for enduring hardship (1:12). Many of James' readers were suffering financial hardship, for this theme is brought up several times (1:9-11, 2:1-6, 5:1-7), indicating that it was one of their prevalent trials.

Sins of Speech

James deals extensively with the issue of one's personal communication (1:26-27, 2:12-13, 3:1-12, 4:11-12, 5:12). The ability to control one's speech in a manner that glorifies God is a mark of true spirituality! The one who considers himself to be religious, but doesn't have control over his tongue is deceived and his religiosity is worthless (1:26). The fact that we stand before God on judgment day should give us a moment of pause regarding the choice of our words (2:12-13). James issues a word of caution to those who teach because they are held to a higher standard (3:1), and considers the one who never commits verbal sins to be the perfect man (3:2). James is very graphic about the destructive potentiality of verbal sins (3:3-12). For instance, words are highly inflammable like a raging forest fire (3:5-6), the inability to control our speech can corrupt the course of one's life (3:6), speech can be demonically inspired (3:8), and the tongue is the most inconsistently used human faculty (3:9-12). One minute we praise the Lord with our words, the next we curse men made in the image of God (3:9-10). That is blatant inconsistency!

James mentions the verbal sins of slander and speaking against other people (4:11-12) as being unacceptable, and a violation of the law. The one who judges his brother is actually guilty of judging the law. The proper thing to do is let God be the judge and not speak against your brothers in Christ that Jesus died for.

James also speaks against insincere oath taking (5:12), by encouraging people to simply say what they mean and mean what they say. In other words, let your yes be yes and your no be no!

The Law

There is a noticeable tension between the writings of Paul and James regarding their views of the law. An understanding of the context from which each author writes is critical to understanding their position on the law (the Old Testament Scriptures). Paul was doing battle against false teachers who were advocating one is saved through faith in Christ and circumcision (Gal 2:15, 5:1-6), hence, Paul sets forth his position that justification is by faith alone (Ro 5:1), not by keeping the works of the law.

Whereas Paul is addressing initial justification, meaning how one enters the body of Christ, James is looking at justification from a different perspective than Paul. James is more concerned about the results of justification by faith, which is a godly lifestyle consisting of good works. One's initial justification by faith is verified by the good works that follow conversion. That's the sense in which James says a man is justified by works, and not faith alone (2:24).

In the book of Galatians, Paul sets forth the position that walking in the Spirit is the fulfillment of the law (Gal 5:18, 23). If the believer lives according to the law, he is living behind the spiritual times. In the current age of Pentecost, the believer walks in the Spirit, and thus, never will violate the intent of the law. Walking in the Spirit fulfills the law, for we are not under the law but grace. Paul, therefore, could be interpreted as having somewhat of a negative view of the law, when in fact he doesn't. He's writing from the post-Pentecost age of the Spirit, where the law has been fulfilled in Christ (Mat 5:17), and a new age of salvation history has arrived with the outpouring of the Spirit. The false teachers insisted that one must keep the law (circumcision, dietary regulations, etc.) in addition to having faith in Christ for salvation, which was totally unacceptable to Paul. Their claim that keeping the law for salvation indicates that they are living in a past era, behind the spiritual times! Paul made it clear that by keeping the law no one will be justified (Gal 2:15-16).

James wrote his homily before these controversies existed that Paul dealt with. He's writing to Jewish Christians, who worshiped in their Jewish context, held the law in high regard, therefore, he is speaking their language by presenting the law as he does. No Jew wants to be considered a lawbreaker (2:9), so he writes as if the believer is to keep the law (2:8), however, James views the royal law (2:8), and the law that gives freedom (2:12) as it is fulfilled in Jesus. He was aware of the new age of salvation history Jesus ushered in with his death and resurrection, and like Paul, was anticipating the Lord's return when this age would come to conclusion, and judgment day would arrive (James 1:12, 3:1, 4:12, 5:1-9). Thus, James presents a positive view of the law, whereas Paul, given his context, seems to present it negatively, when in fact he really isn't! Understanding the background from which each author writes helps to resolve the tension between James and Paul.

Wisdom

The Jews view wisdom as a quality of spiritual life! Wisdom isn't intelligence, such as having the ability to grasp abstract concepts, or possessing a high IQ. The wise person has the ability to live out the Scriptures in everyday life! Hence, wisdom is very practical in nature not theoretical. The wise man reflects his wisdom in his lifestyle. The Jews were practical utilitarian people, who thought that knowledge of Scripture would give them wisdom for everyday practical matters. The book of Proverbs and James are complimentary in nature and are great books to study in tandem.

Paul speaks of the fruit of the Spirit and lists a number of virtues that the Holy Spirit produces in the believer. James speaks of the wisdom from above, and lists a number of wisdom-virtues. I believe both authors are saying the same thing, but in different terminology. Paul speaks of the post-Pentecost work of the Spirit bearing fruit in the believer (Gal 5:22-23), whereas James sees wisdom-virtues produced in the life of a believer (James 3:17-18). Certainly, James would agree with Paul that the Spirit produces the virtues he lists in Galatians. Likewise, Paul would agree with the list of James' wisdom-virtues that have their origin from above (the Holy Spirit). Wisdom is a key concept in Jewish thought-life, so James is speaking the language of his Jewish audience by bringing wisdom into his writing. For this reason I have chosen to subtitle this book "James: Wisdom in Action"!

Repentance

Things were not neat and tidy in James' congregations! There were fights, quarrels and battles going on in his churches (3:13-18, 4:1-2), which was an indication that their spirituality was suspect! They have become worldly and placed themselves in a position to receive chastisement from above. James will have no worldliness among his congregations, and calls for repentance (4:4-10). Becoming worldly is depicted as a form of spiritual adultery (4:4), for the church is the bride of Christ, and must remain faithful to her Lord!

The solution to worldliness and corrupt spirituality is to repent by submitting to God, and resisting the Devil (4:7). Believers living with one foot in the world, and the other foot in the church is unacceptable to James. He calls for whole-hearted devotion, and humility before God. James 4:1-10, provides some of the best teaching in all of Scripture on the topic of repentance.

James and Jesus

James had familiarity with Jesus' teaching. As his brother, it should not surprise us that James would be familiar with some of the dominant themes that Jesus taught. Much of Jesus' teaching in the Sermon on the Mount is reflected in James' homily, which the following comparison illustrates:

Mathew 5:11-12: "Blessed are you when people insult you, persecute you and falsely say all kinds of evil against you because of me. [12]Rejoice and be glad, because great is your reward in heaven, for in the same way they persecuted the prophets who were before you.

Compared with

James 1:2: Consider it pure joy, my brothers and sisters, whenever you face trials of many kinds

Matthew 6:14-15: For if you forgive other people when they sin against you, your heavenly Father will also forgive you. [15]But if you do not forgive others their sins, your Father will not forgive your sins.

Compared with

James 2:12-13: Speak and act as those who are going to be judged by the law that gives freedom, [13]because judgment without mercy will be shown to anyone who has not been merciful. Mercy triumphs over judgment.

Matthew 7:16-20: By their fruit you will recognize them. Do people pick grapes from thornbushes, or figs from thistles? [17]Likewise, every good tree bears good fruit, but a bad tree bears bad fruit. [18]A good tree cannot bear bad fruit, and a bad tree cannot bear good fruit. [19]Every tree that does not bear good fruit is cut down and thrown into the fire. [20]Thus, by their fruit you will recognize them.

Compared With

James 3:11-12: Can both fresh water and salt water flow from the same spring? [12]My brothers and sisters, can a fig tree bear olives, or a grapevine bear figs? Neither can a salt spring produce fresh water.

Matthew 5:34-37: But I tell you, do not swear an oath at all: either by heaven, for it is God's throne; [35]or by the earth, for it is his footstool; or by Jerusalem, for it is the city of the Great King. [36]And do not swear by your head, for you cannot make even one hair white or black. [37]All you need to say is simply 'Yes' or 'No'; anything beyond this comes from the evil one.

Compared With

James 5:12: Above all, my brothers and sisters, do not swear—not by heaven or by earth or by anything else. All you need to say is a simple "Yes" or "No." Otherwise you will be condemned.

Jesus and James also share similar ethical teachings in that the Shema (Deu 6:4-5) and Leviticus 19:18 seem to take center stage in their teachings. On one occasion when Jesus was asked what the greatest command of the law was he responded in the following way recorded in Matthew 22:37-40:

> Jesus replied: "'Love the Lord your God with all your heart and with all your soul and with all your mind.' 38This is the first and greatest commandment. 39And the second is like it: 'Love your neighbor as yourself.' 40All the Law and the Prophets hang on these two commandments."

Jesus quoted the Shema (Deu 6:5) identifying it as the first and greatest command, then added the second "Love your neighbor as yourself", which was a quote from Leviticus 19:18. So central to the life of a disciple are these two commands, that the law and prophets are fulfilled as the believer obeys the love commands of Jesus. This is central to the ethical requirements of discipleship for the Lord Jesus.

James follows Jesus in his ethical teachings. In 2:8 James said: "If you really keep the royal law found in Scripture, "Love your neighbor as yourself," you are doing right." Two things are noteworthy in this verse. First, James' reference to "royal law" refers to the law as it is fulfilled in Jesus. The Lord said he didn't come to abolish the law and prophets, but to fulfill them

(Mat 5:17). James sees the royal law, and the law that gives freedom (2:12), as being fulfilled in the Christ event, so James wasn't living behind the eschatological times. James was fully aware of the new era that Christ ushered in with his death and resurrection, and was looking forward to the end of the age at Christ's return (1:12, 2:13, 3:1, 4:11-12, 5:1, 7-8).

Secondly, James identifies the royal law as "Love your neighbor as yourself", which is from Leviticus 19:18. James is certainly tracking with Jesus in his ethical requirements for discipleship. Like Jesus, James draws from Leviticus 19:18; in fact, a good case can be made for James drawing heavily on Leviticus 19 in writing this entire homily. Many of the themes he develops can be traced back to Leviticus 19:12-18. Note the following similarities:

Lev 19:12: Do not swear falsely by my name and so profane the name of your God. I am the LORD.

Compared with

James 5:12: Above all, my brothers and sisters, do not swear— not by heaven or by earth or by anything else. All you need to say is a simple "Yes" or "No." Otherwise you will be condemned.

Lev 19:13: Do not defraud or rob your neighbor. Do not hold back the wages of a hired worker overnight.

Compared with

James 5:4: Look! The wages you failed to pay the workers who mowed your fields are crying out against you. The cries of the harvesters have reached the ears of the Lord Almighty.

Lev 19:14: "'Do not curse the deaf or put a stumbling block in front of the blind, but fear your God. I am the LORD.

Compared with

James 1:27: Religion that God our Father accepts as pure and faultless is this: to look after orphans and widows in their distress and to keep oneself from being polluted by the world.

Lev 19:15: Do not pervert justice; do not show partiality to the poor or favoritism to the great, but judge your neighbor fairly.

Compared with

James 2:1: My brothers and sisters, believers in our glorious Lord Jesus Christ must not show favoritism.

Lev 19:16: Do not go about spreading slander among your people. "'Do not do anything that endangers your neighbor's life. I am the LORD.

Compared with

James 4:11-12: Brothers and sisters, do not slander one another. Anyone who speaks against a brother or sister or judges them speaks against the law and judges it. When you judge the law, you are not keeping it, but sitting in judgment on it. [12]There is only one Lawgiver and Judge, the one who is able to save and destroy. But you—who are you to judge your neighbor?

Lev 19:17: Do not hate your brother in your heart. Rebuke your neighbor frankly so you will not share in his guilt.

Compared with

James 4:1-2: What causes fights and quarrels among you? Don't they come from your desires that battle within you? [2]You desire but do not have, so you kill. You covet but you cannot get what you want, so you quarrel and fight. You do not have because you do not ask God.

Lev 19:18: Do not seek revenge or bear a grudge against anyone among your people, but love your neighbor as yourself. I am the LORD.

Compared with

James 2:8: If you really keep the royal law found in Scripture, "Love your neighbor as yourself," you are doing right.

In conclusion, James' ethical standards are similar to those set forth by the Lord Jesus, and testify to his familiarity with Jesus' teachings. James' ethical focus was through the lens of the Shema (James 3:19), and Leviticus 19, as was Jesus'. James was greatly influenced by Leviticus 19 in writing this homily, to the extent that the Leviticus chapter shaped much of his sermon.

Significance for Today

The church should take this book of the Bible to heart! We live in a world that is filled with hurting, disenfranchised people that need the compassion and mercy of others. In the Chicago area, where I live, there are homeless people roaming the streets, and scores of people are out of work needing financial help. The church must rise to the challenge and love their neighbor as themselves!

Living in the prosperous West, believers in America are influenced by all the trappings of the world system, which can prove to be hazardous to one's spiritual health! James' appeal for no nonsense Christianity should challenge the Western church! Its utility and practicality make it one of the most popular books of the Bible to believers around the world. However, in the scholarly community James hasn't gotten the attention he deserves. For instance, there are no direct references to the Holy Spirit in James' homily (with the possible exception of 4:5), which caused Martin Luther to conclude that James is an epistle of straw! Scholars tend to view James as lacking theological substance, and basically place James on the bottom of the list in terms of theological thinkers.

Considering the place that James occupied in the leadership of the early church he should get more attention, but he has been relegated to a place below Paul, Peter, John and others. James emerged as the first pastor of the mother church in Jerusalem, from where the Christian movement began. The Jerusalem church was the epicenter from which shockwaves went throughout the Roman Empire registering high on the spiritual Richter scale. James was the leader of God's new work in the world centered in Jerusalem. He stood heads above the others and was an icon in the early church.

Galatians 2:9 lists James first as one of the pillars of the church. The Jerusalem council (Acts 15) played a huge role in heading off a major controversy regarding Gentile inclusion into the church. There were some spiritual heavyweights in attendance like Peter, Paul, and Barnabas, but it was James who had the final word! When Paul came to Jerusalem on his last visit (Acts 21:18) he reported to James and the elders. It appears that everybody reported to James, for he was clearly recognized as the leader of the mother church!

The tide is turning, and the scholarly community has a renewed interest in James, so perhaps he will get the attention that he rightfully deserves. Whether he does or not, the book of James offers the reader a glimpse into vital Christianity from a spiritual heavyweight—Jesus' brother and the pastor of the mother church in Jerusalem. When thinking about possible titles for this book I came up with a number of ideas, one of which was "No Nonsense Christianity"! Although I didn't choose this title, it would be a fitting description of what James sets forth regarding the life of a disciple of Christ! I hope that all believers will profit from studying the book of James, and go on to live a life of "no nonsense Christianity."

CHAPTER ONE

"THE GREETING"

James 1:1

James, a servant of God and of the Lord Jesus Christ, to the twelve tribes scattered among the nations: Greetings.

In this brief introduction to his letter James reveals much about his humility, how he views his relationship to his brother—the Lord Jesus, and how he views the twelve tribes of Israel.

James, a servant of God and of the Lord Jesus Christ, to the twelve tribes scattered among the nations: Greetings. (1:1)

The author of this letter is James—the Lord's brother (see introduction). Initially, James wasn't a believer when Jesus was conducting his ministry, however he became a believer some time after Jesus' crucifixion, and established himself as a key leader in the early church in Jerusalem.

Given the fact that James grew up having Jesus as his big brother, he would have some unique insights about Jesus that nobody else could possibly have. How many people get to say their big brother was the Lord Jesus Christ! He has firsthand knowledge of Jesus' character that few people would have. He could boldly assert that he knows more about Jesus than any other disciple because he grew up with him. Jog your imagination for a moment, and think of boyhood stories that James could tell people about Jesus. In fact, the two of them may have even borne a physical resemblance.

Rather than identifying himself as the Lord's brother, he refers to himself as a "servant of God and of the Lord Jesus Christ". The word servant is more literally translated slave (*doulos*). In the ancient world slavery was common, with over half the people in the Roman Empire living in that condition. Slaves were property of their Masters, who had complete control over them, even to the point of putting them to death if they desired.

The fact that James calls himself the "slave of God" and of the Lord Jesus Christ is a reflection of his humility, and his deep loyalty to his Master—Jesus. Many Christians were slaves, so James' identification of himself as a slave would hit home to his audience. It was considered an honor by Christians to be considered the slave of Jesus.

The title "Lord Jesus Christ" is a high and lofty title. "Lord" is a translation of the Greek word *kurios*, which was used in the Septuagint (the Greek translation of the Hebrew Scripture) to translate *YHWH,* God's name as it was revealed to Moses. That *kurios* is Jesus, and *kurios* is *YHWH* indicates that Jesus is God! Not only does "Lord" testify to Jesus' deity, it is also a description of Jesus in his exalted position at the right hand of God the Father, from where we await his return.

The name "Jesus" reminds us of his humanity. God came to earth and added humanity to his deity (Luke 1:35, Heb 2:17), thus identifying with our condition. The name Jesus is the

Greek form of the Hebrew Joshua, which literally means *YHWH saves*. Jesus would die on the cross, thus paving the way for our salvation and reconciliation with God. Therefore, inherent in the name Jesus is his mission statement: God Saves through Jesus Christ.

The title "Christ" is a translation of the Greek word *christos,* which literally means the Anointed One, or the Messiah. Christ is the Messiah sent by God to atone for our sins, and usher in a new age of salvation history.

In summary, the title "Lord Jesus Christ" testifies to his deity, his exalted position at the right hand of God, his humanity, and his role as the Messiah. To call Jesus Lord in the First Century was dangerous to the one making the profession of faith. To the Jews it was blasphemy to call any man Lord, and to the Romans it was considered a treasonous affront to the authority of the Emperor. Many believers were persecuted and even put to death for making the profession "Jesus is Lord"!

This letter has an obvious Jewish flavor, which is reflected to the addressee—"the twelve tribes scattered among the nations". The ten tribes that constituted the Northern Kingdom were deported by the Assyrians and ceased to exist as identifiable people groups. Those who remained in the land interbred with non-Jews and were considered half-breeds—the Samaritans. There was great animosity between the Southern tribes of Judea and Benjamin toward the Samaritans, and at various times in their history civil war broke out between the North and South.

The prophets foretold that there would be a re-gathering of all 12 tribes in the end times, which would result in a restoration of the nation of Israel. By writing to the 12 tribes James is reminding these Jewish Christians of their heritage, while at the same time establishing their identity as the new Israel—the church. Through Christ there has been a restoration of Israel in the sense that there is a new group of redeemed people in God's program—the church—which one becomes part of through faith in Christ. This doesn't mean that God has no agenda for today's nation of Israel, James is just pointing out that God has done something new in the creation of the church, of which James' readers are a part.

Due to the persecution of Jewish Christians at the hands of Saul, they were forced to flee Jerusalem and relocate outside of Palestine (Acts 8:1-4, 11:19). They were exiled from their homeland, and in a sense, seem to be following in the footsteps of their ancestors, who were also exiled at different times in their history. Thus, James introduces the theme of God's people living in exile away from their homeland, and away from their true spiritual home—heaven. The church is not confined to a specific geographic location as the Israelites were in the Promised Land. The church is transnational and global in scope, but the true home of the church is heaven!

The trials that would result from a group of people living as refugees would be overwhelming! James was writing to people who were living in crisis mode, and wants to give them encouragement and support as their pastor. His compassion and tender heart is very evident throughout this homily.

He offers them his "greeting". This is the Greek word *chairein,* which was a common greeting in the secular world. The word means more than just "hello", it carries with it the meaning of being joyful, or being glad. It is written as a present infinitive in Greek, which denotes non-stop, continuous action. Thus, James is saying keep on being joyful, and he sets the stage for his discussion of how the believer should cope with trials by "considering them pure joy" (1:2). The word James uses in v. 2 for joy, is a variation of the same word (greeting) used here in v. 1.

Insights and Application, (v. 1)

The contemporary church has its fair share of celebrities and high profile people. Billy Graham, Charles Stanley, Chuck Swindoll, and many others are well known in the Christian community, having impeccable reputations. Thank God for those people who have had fruitful ministries, having provided a great example for all to emulate. Unfortunately, there have been many Christian celebrities that had huge ministries, were well known around the world, and had their ministries come to a screeching halt because of moral failures, financial improprieties, and so forth. Success can go to your head! Proverbs 16:18 says: Pride goes before destruction, a haughty spirit before a fall.

A good friend of mine that I attended seminary with was on the pastoral staff of a church in Korea that had 70,000 members! Wow, that's huge! He said in a big church like that with ornate state of the art facilities, lots of money, and people who treat you with great respect, it's easy to begin to think you're something special, and it can go to your head! When someone is in the limelight, getting all kinds of praise and accolades from the people it can make them proud! One can become intoxicated with delusions of grandeur, and the potential for falling from grace is very real!

Given the familial proximity that James has to Jesus, one might think that James would be prone to boast about his relationship with the Lord, and call attention to himself. He could make prideful claims that his knowledge of Jesus surpasses that of any other disciple, and in a sense he would be justified in saying that! The Savior of the world was James' half-brother, which probably drew a lot of attention to him. It would not be uncommon for people to ask him questions about what it was like to grow up with Jesus, and ask him to share a memorable story about the Lord. Perhaps, James had a great deal of notoriety, even celebrity status because he was Jesus' brother, and the pastor of the first church in Jerusalem. Believers may have gone out-of-their-way to meet James just because they wanted to meet the brother of Jesus, and shake his hand! One can see how this could tend to make James prideful, however, evidence of pridefulness in James is nowhere to be found in his homily!

James could have begun his letter in the following ways:

James, the pastor of the first church in history!

James, the younger brother of Jesus!

James, the one has more spiritual insights about Jesus than anybody in the world!

James, close associate of Peter, John, Paul, and the other apostles!

James, the one who has a special "in" with the Lord Jesus!

He could have thrown all kinds of titles on the table to impress his readers, and laid it on really thick, however, he didn't do that! He simply chose the designation James, the servant (slave) of God and the Lord Jesus Christ.

In spite of James' relationship to Jesus, it didn't make him arrogant such that he derailed in his ministry like many other high profile people. He maintained humility and served as an exemplary leader in the early church, thus providing a great example of humility for disciples of all time to follow.

CHAPTER TWO

"COPING WITH TRIALS"

James 1:2-8

Consider it pure joy, my brothers and sisters, whenever you face trials of many kinds, ³because you know that the testing of your faith produces perseverance. ⁴Let perseverance finish its work so that you may be mature and complete, not lacking anything. ⁵If any of you lacks wisdom, you should ask God, who gives generously to all without finding fault, and it will be given to you. ⁶But when you ask, you must believe and not doubt, because the one who doubts is like a wave of the sea, blown and tossed by the wind. ⁷That person should not expect to receive anything from the Lord. ⁸Such a person is double-minded and unstable in all they do.

Nobody likes to go through trials! It's much easier to sit back and enjoy life rather than suffer hardships because of your stand with the Lord Jesus. Disciples of Christ should accept the fact that trials are a normal part of life, and understand that God does special things in his people to facilitate their growth when going through challenges. James discusses many of the tangible spiritual benefits that accrue to the believer by going through trials such as: strengthened faith, increased stamina, deeper maturity, acquisition of wisdom, and a deepened prayer life. While going through difficult times disciples need to face trials with a fresh perspective that embraces the challenge— looking for the positive results, rather than wallowing in negativity and despair.

Consider it pure joy, my brothers and sisters, whenever you face trials of many kinds, [3]because you know that the testing of your faith produces perseverance. (1:2-3)

James' readers were living in the midst of many and varied trials, which he tells them to consider pure joy. A more normal response to living in dire circumstances would be to complain, be filled with self-pity, and be grumpy! Thus, James' command to be joyful seems like an unnatural response to the difficult circumstances they faced. Trials are not things that people consider to be joyful experiences. James is calling for his readers to entertain a different perspective of trials for reasons that will unfold throughout this passage. The diversity of trials that life presented to his readers was many and varied, just as the modern-day believer faces a multiplicity of trials. These new Christians were persecuted, forced to leave their homes, suffered economic hardship, and much more.

Viewing their trials from a spiritual perspective requires intentional thought and deliberation. When a believer understands the positive role that trials play in his spiritual development, it then becomes clear why James says trials can be considered to be pure joy.

James will repeatedly (1:2, 16, 19; 2:1, 5, 14; 3:10, 12; 4:11; 5:7, 9, 10, 12, 19) refer to his readers as "brothers and sisters", which is a translation of the Greek word *adelphoi.* Since it is masculine plural it could be translated "brothers" referring to just men, however it is clear that James is referring to both men and women that comprise the family of God. He uses this terminology to express his tender heart toward the people, and identify with his audience as a fellow member of the God's family.

When enduring a trial your faith is tested! Faith is an essential ingredient in the Christian experience. We grow in our faith by learning to trust God in difficult circumstances, and moment-by-moment, situation-by-situation depend on the Lord. As the believer experiences trials the test is whether or not he will continue to attend church, study Scripture, seek the fellowship and support of other believers, continue to pray, and be faithful to the Lord. Some believers may quit under the duress of hardship! Discouragement may become so intense that they become dropouts and suffer spiritual shipwreck regarding their faith.

The word for testing is *dokimion,* which is a word that describes a process of determining the genuineness or authenticity of an item. One usage of this word was to describe the process of establishing the genuineness and purity of metals. When metals are melted by intense heat, the impurities will float to the top of the caldron, and would be removed with a ladle, thus leaving pure alloy. This process would determine the genuineness of the metal.

When a believer goes through the process of a trial and successfully endures it, they are proving their faith in Christ to be authentic. The heat of the trial burns the impurities of doubt and double-mindedness out of one's faith, such that faith is strengthened and purified. This is a positive experience in the believer's life and should be reason to rejoice. Arriving at this conclusion takes some deliberation about the nature of trails, and requires the ability to consider them from a spiritual perspective.

Another reason why trials should be considered a source of joy is "that the testing of your faith produces perseverance". There are many virtues that Christians are to develop, but James identifies the highly useful trait of perseverance (*hupomone*). This is a compound word in Greek: *hupo* means under, and *mone* means remain. Literally, *hupomone* means to "remain under." The meaning of the word is to persevere, endure, and remain steadfast. This is not a passive activity where the believer tries to go around the trial, or sit back and wait for the challenge to pass. This is a quality in a believer, which enables him to embrace the trial and face it head on with tenacity and prevail. For this reason, I prefer the translation "spiritual stamina" rather than perseverance. Going through trials gives disciples endurance and spiritual stamina, in the same way that athletes develop stamina in their training routines.

Trials make us spiritually tough, and enable believers to stay the course with the Lord without walking away from Him. In sports, some people have to come out of the game, and sit on the bench so they can catch their breath and drink some Gatorade. They are not as well conditioned as their teammates. They need to do more conditioning drills to increase their stamina so they can stay in the game. In the Christian arena, enduring trials increases our spiritual stamina and builds our faith. These are reasons to rejoice when trials come our way. God is using them to do a work in us and improve our character. We are growing as Christians, which is something to be joyful about.

Let perseverance finish its work so that you may be mature and complete, not lacking anything. (1:4)

The fruit of perseverance in the believer is the development of a mature character. Trials are a vehicle through which disciples' of Christ grow to maturity in the faith. As the believer develops spiritual stamina he is also becoming a mature Christian with strong faith. The Greek word translated mature is *teleios,* which can be translated perfect, complete, or mature. The word is found twice in this verse: Perseverance must finish (*teleios*) its work so that you may be mature (*teleios*) and complete, not lacking anything.

We become mature by going through the diversity of trials that life may present to us. We have weaknesses and imperfections that can become strengths and virtues by going through trials. A wealth of life experience is gained by enduring trials, and these experiences lend themselves to developing a Christlike character.

Perseverance also does its work so that we are "not lacking anything". As we go through trials we develop life skills, gain experience, and become wise, so that we can cope with the challenges that life presents to us. The New Living Translation does a great job in capturing the nuances of the Greek words in its translation: So let it grow, for when your endurance is fully developed, you will be strong in character and ready for anything.

When we think of the mature Christians that we know, it should make us mindful of what it took for them to get to their place of maturity and seasoning. They have suffered many trials, but it is those challenges of life that helped produce the Christlike character that they so adequately display, and that we may envy. This is another reason why the believer should consider trials a source of joy—God is using them to mold us into seasoned believers.

If any of you lacks wisdom, you should ask God, who gives generously to all without finding fault, and it will be given to you. (1:5)

When going through a trial the questions people often ask themselves are: What should I do? How does God want me to respond? How can I discern what God's will is for me in this challenge I'm facing? How should I pray about this? Answers to these questions require wisdom, which James sees as a key ingredient in coping with trials.

Enduring trials has a way of increasing the frequency of prayer in a believer's life. Difficult circumstances have a way of bringing us to our knees in prayer and humility. One of the things to be prayed for is wisdom. As God imparts wisdom to us, answers to the above questions are answered (Pro 2:6, 12). The promise of God to the believer in this passage is that as we ask for wisdom, God will give it to us generously and will not heap condemnation on us for asking. This promise is for all believers regardless of our level of maturity or social status. There is no guilt trip that God lays on us as we come to the throne of grace for help. He embraces us and will impart wisdom to us, but he doesn't say when answers to our questions will come, so believers must be diligent in prayer.

But when you ask, you must believe and not doubt, because the one who doubts is like a wave of the sea, blown and tossed by the wind. ⁷That person should not expect to receive anything from the Lord. ⁸Such a person is double-minded and unstable in all they do. (1:6-8)

Moving from the content of the prayer request, which was wisdom, James addresses the manner in which we should pray: "he must believe and not doubt." Prayer should be done with a high level of faith that God is hearing our prayer, and that He will answer according to his will. The one who prays with a high level of doubt is compared to a man who is like the "wave of the sea, blown and tossed by the wind." James uses a number of colorful word pictures to illustrate his points throughout his letter. This image of the sea constantly in motion, always changing, never appearing the same is a picture of instability—not unwavering trust in the Lord. This is a picture of a believer who does not possess single-minded faith, but is inconsistent and all over the map regarding his prayer life. There is constant motion between faith and doubt, trust and skepticism, and moment-by-moment faith shifting to moment-by-moment indecision and doubt.

James sends a grave warning to the one who has this inconsistent faith in his prayer life by telling him that he "should not think he will receive anything from the Lord". If we talk to God with that type of inconsistency, we can't expect to consistently hear from God. The key ingredient to having our prayers answered, that James stresses for us, is that prayer must be offered in the medium of faith. There is evidence in the Scripture to support James assertion of the primacy of faith in prayer (Mat 7:7-11, Mark 11:22-24). Prayer is most fruitful in the rich soil of unwavering faith.

James also describes the doubter as a "double-minded man, unstable in all they do" (v. 8). This type of prayer life is a reflection of a man who is a walking contradiction. Like trying to go in opposite directions at the same time is one who prays with double-mindedness. This is a picture of someone who is conflicted! They pray with faith one moment, then shift gears to doubt the next moment. They move from a healthy expectation of hearing from God, to a skeptical doubt of whether or not He even exists! They advocate discipleship yet embrace sin! The conflicted man is one who is lacking peace in his life, and is all over the spiritual map!

This deficiency in prayer reflects something else about the person in question; namely he is "unstable in all he does". This instability is proof that perseverance hasn't done its work in the person's life, and he hasn't come to be a mature Christian. Inconsistency in one's prayer life translates to other areas of life as well. We live in an age where faith is watered down, such that many live a nominal Christian life, worldliness permeates the body of Christ, and churchgoers are increasingly confronted with their inconsistent lifestyle.

Insights and Application (1:2-8)

This passage speaks to everybody's heart because we all go through trials—big and small! James wrote this homily to a group of people that were living in crisis mode, which for many contemporary believers is where they live as well. Coping with trials is always difficult so James provides his readers with helpful advice. Nobody considers trials to be joyful from the natural perspective, but when looked at from an eternal perspective one can gain insights as to why we can rejoice in challenging circumstances.

God will do a work in your life by molding, refining your faith, strengthening you, developing your prayer life, and bringing you to maturity in Christ through the trials that you face. God uses trials to bring his people to maturity! That is one of the basic ways in which God develops us as disciples' of Christ. For that reason, believers can rejoice when trials enter their lives. They will experience spiritual growth, and God will reveal himself in fresh ways. Just as steel is hardened in the forgery, the believer's faith is forged in the crucible of trials.

James would disagree with some of the popular teachings in contemporary Christendom, which imply that believers can always be healthy, prosperous, and living a comfortable lifestyle if they have the faith to believe God for those things. James' position is that trials are a normal part of a disciple's life. This is a hard pill to swallow! The normative experience for all believers is to go through trials that test our faith! James challenges us to see the good side of it from a spiritual perspective.

Building spiritual stamina, like developing physical stamina isn't always fun, nor is it easy. Jerry Kramer played right guard for the Green Bay Packers under coach Vince Lombardi. He described the summer training camps as brutal. With rising temperatures and soaring humidity, coach Lombardi would push his players to their physical and mental limits. Players would lie on the grass gasping for air at the end of conditioning drills, as they tried to recover for the next exercise. Kramer said Lombardi would push you until he got everything out of you that he could get, and more!

Brutal as those workouts were they paid high dividends. The Packers won three consecutive world championships, including the first two Super Bowls! Coach Lombardi imposed a brutal training schedule on his players, but their conditioning gave them an edge over their opponents. In the spiritual arena, when God imposes a trial on your life, even though it may be painful, that trial gives you an edge in your spiritual development! Trials develop spiritual stamina, which is something that every believer needs, just as every athlete needs to have physical stamina.

We've all seen under-conditioned athletes, who need to come out of the game, sit on the bench, take oxygen, and drink Gatorade. Their contribution to the team suffers because they aren't properly conditioned. God uses trials that come into our lives to build spiritual endurance, so we can get off the bench and back on the playing field of serving in ministry! Trials give us an edge in serving God!

CHAPTER THREE

"THE TRIAL OF POVERTY"

James 1:9-11

Believers in humble circumstances ought to take pride in their high position. ¹⁰But the rich should take pride in their humiliation—since they will pass away like a wild flower. ¹¹For the sun rises with scorching heat and withers the plant; its blossom falls and its beauty is destroyed. In the same way, the rich will fade away even while they go about their business.

The vast majority of James readers were dirt poor. He is identifying with their plight in life and trying to encourage them to keep their heads up and press on. No doubt many people suffered economic hardship as they were forced to flee their homes and relocate outside of Jerusalem. Some of these folks probably were at one time well off, but lost everything as they were forced to leave. They had to face the trial of poverty and consider it a source of joy for the reasons mentioned above. This is a double whammy, in that to suffer a drastic decrease in your standard of living is painful enough, but at the same time to consider it a source of joy is a real challenge! This is the first specific trial that James mentions.

Believers in humble circumstances ought to take pride in their high position. [10]But the rich should take pride in their humiliation—since they will pass away like a wild flower. (1:9-10)

The brother in humble circumstances is the disciple of Christ who is poor. Of interest is the fact that James says the poor brother should take pride in his high position, which is contrasted with the rich Christian (v. 10) who is told to take pride in his low position. In the world's way of thinking the poor man would not be viewed as being in a high position! It is the rich man who would be considered to be in the high position. James has reversed the values of the world's way of viewing poverty and wealth and put them in a spiritual perspective. The poor man is in the high position and the rich man is in the low position.

World's Perspective on Poverty and Wealth

Poor Christian
Nothing to be proud about
He is in a low position

Rich Christian
Take pride
He is in a high position

James' Role Reversal on Poverty and Wealth

Poor Christian
Take pride
In his high position

Rich Christian
Take pride
In his humiliation

Why should the poor man take pride in his high position? Those who don't have an abundance of material possessions are in a position where they have to live by faith, and trust God to meet their needs. They have no other option but to live by faith because every day is an exercise of trusting the Lord to have their daily needs met. James considered this to be a high position in life. He will later say: "Listen, my dear brothers and sisters: Has not God chosen those who are poor in the eyes of the world to be rich in faith and to inherit the kingdom he promised those who love him (2:5)?"

The poor believer should "take pride" (*kauchaomai*) in his high position in life. The range of meaning of this Greek word includes the concepts of to rejoice, glory, or boast. Although the poor believer may suffer material deprivation in this life he can boast of his high place of being a child of God, totally dependent on his heavenly Father, who gives good gifts to those who ask and has committed Himself to taking care of His children (Mat 6:31-34, 7:11).

On the other side of the fence is the rich believer who "should take pride in his humiliation". In what sense is he in a low position, and why would he boast about that? Unlike the poor man, he doesn't have to trust God for his daily needs and live moment-by-moment by faith. James considers this a low position. He has enough money to buy all the food, possessions, and luxury items that his heart desires. James isn't saying that there is anything wrong with money; it is morally neutral. It is the attitude that people attach to money that can be the root of all sorts of evil (1 Tim 6:10). During a trial the rich man can't trust in his riches, he has to direct his faith to the Lord Jesus.

For example, when a severe sickness presents itself, all the money in the world can't restore a person's health. When a person is lacking the peace of God money can't buy that. When tragedy strikes and we suffer the loss of a loved one, money can't buy that person back to life. Thus, the rich man has to divert his attention away from his financial security and find his security through faith in God. This is the sense in which he is to boast of his low position; he is forced to step away from his financial portfolio and come lower to meet Christ and discover the riches that he has in his spiritual portfolio, as he copes with his trials.

...since they will pass away like a wild flower. For the sun rises with scorching heat and withers the plant; its blossom falls and its beauty is destroyed. In the same way, the rich man will fade away even while they go about their business. (1:10b-11)

When trials enter the life of a person who is well off, he is challenged to understand that his riches can't solve all of life's problems. Trials make him aware that all his riches are transitory and he can't take them to heaven when he dies. In fact, James says it's not the rich man's possessions that are transitory, it's the rich man himself who is transitory, for "he will pass away like a wild flower" (v.10b). Life is short, as is the lifespan of a wild flower, which may last a day-or-two. In the brief time that a man may amass a fortune, he is no different than the poor man in that both succumb to the brevity of life.

James further develops his point by utilizing the imagery from Isaiah 40:6-8:

> A voice says, "Cry out." And I said, "What shall I cry?" "All people are like grass, and all their faithfulness is like the flowers of the field. ⁷The grass withers and the flowers fall, because the breath of the LORD blows on them. Surely the people are grass. ⁸The grass withers and the flowers fall, but the word of our God endures forever."

The hot sun scorches the flowers and their once beautiful look is gone forever. They are here today and gone tomorrow! The rich man's possessions are like the flowers that fade away. The man who amasses wealth dies just like the poor man; there is no difference. The point James is making is that as the rich man is busy enterprising and making money his life can suddenly, without warning, come to an end. His money can't prevent this from happening, and he can't take the fruit of his labor with him into the next life. Although he may have great influence and clout in his society, his money doesn't enable him to control all the variables of life, especially the moment of his death.

The rich man and the poor man are both equal in the eyes of God. The poor believer is already rich in Christ, the rich believer whose earthly riches will one day disappear, needs to learn humility, and focus on the true riches of heaven, where his inheritance lies for all eternity.

Whether you are rich or poor, trials place all believers on a level playing field and bring us to a greater dependence upon the Lord. Many of the believers, rich and poor, were being persecuted for their faith. Their money didn't exempt them from partaking of the sufferings of Christ (Phil 3:10).

Insights and Application, (1:9-11)

When we go to church and pull into the parking lot we see a variety of cars; foreign and domestic, high end and entry level, new and used ones fill the parking lot. This is a reminder that some believers have more money than others. What is our attitude to those who are blessed financially? Do we envy them? Are we angry at them? Do we feel like they are better off than we are?

James challenges us to not be envious of those who have more than we do. He has told us that the poor believer is in a very high place in the eyes of God. He reversed the value system of the world's way of thinking which is: rich is better than poor. James says no, the poor man is in a higher place than the rich man.

If you are the brother who has been blessed financially, there may be a tendency to be proud of your material wealth and adopt the world's view of thinking that you are in the high place of our society. Perhaps, you may think that you have some special favor with God that others don't have! Maybe you are influenced by the prosperity gospel that says that the fruit of spiritual maturity is material prosperity. Maybe you've been conned into thinking that your possessions are evidence of your spiritual maturity and special favor with God, over and above other believers who have less than you.

James tries to undo this mentality by reminding the rich man that he is in a low position in the eyes of God, because he can't take it with him. His money doesn't enable him to have control over all the variables of life. The rich may have more options for enjoying the comforts of this world, but they can't escape tragedy, sickness, natural disasters, and ultimately death. The rich man may be very industrious, have a great work ethic, and a good head for business, but could at any moment drop over dead of a heart attack. What good did his money and his 60 hour work-week do for him then?

Either way, whether rich or poor, believers need to develop humble dependence on the Lord in their trials. Both poverty and wealth are trials to be endured and tests of character. The majority of people are in the category of being in humble circumstances and we may tend to look at those who are well-off like their life is so much easier than ours. We may think they are immune to trials that we go through. This is very wrong thinking! Rich people have trials just like poor people, but they are different. God loves the rich believer as much as he loves the poor believer, but desires that both come to maturity in Christ through humble dependence on Him.

CHAPTER FOUR

"THE REWARD"

James 1:12

Blessed is the one who perseveres under trial because, having stood the test, that person will receive the crown of life that God has promised to those who love him.

God is gracious and rewards his people for their faithfulness. There are rewards in store for all believers who endure trials and prove the authenticity of their faith in Christ. The people James was writing to were going through hardships and he wants them to know that even though they are poor, and many may have been well off at one time but lost everything, there is a reward waiting for them in the future. If they endure the trials and remain faithful to Christ it will all be worth the suffering they went through because God has a great blessing for them.

Blessed is the one who perseveres under trial because, having stood the test, that person will receive the crown of life that God has promised to those who love him. (1:12)

"Blessed" is the translation of the word *makarios,* which also means happy and fortunate, and reminds us of Jesus' words in the beatitudes in the Sermon on the Mount (Mat 5). The one who knows the Lord is considered in Scripture to be in a blessed position. The one who endures trials, remains faithful to Christ and passes the testing of his faith (1:3) is the one who receives the crown of life (Rev 2:10).

This believer has successfully accomplished the content of vv. 2-5 in all the trials that came into his life. His faith has been proven authentic and genuine because he didn't deviate from the straight and narrow path of Christ. Even in the midst of persecution and suffering hardship for Christ he remained faithful to the Lord. He has developed his faith, spiritual stamina, and came to be a mature believer.

The crown is the *stephanos*, which was the laurel wreath awarded to the victors of athletic contests in the Greek world. The crown is the symbol of spiritual victory. The reward is eschatological in nature, not temporal. The crown is thought by many to be eternal life. Grammatically it is correct to translate "the crown of life" as the "crown which is eternal life." Great debate exists in the church today regarding the status of the five crowns mentioned Scripture (2 Tim 4:8, 1 Thess 2:19, 1 Pet 5:4, 1 Cor 9:26, Rev 2:10). Some take the position they are separate rewards that the believer is eligible to earn throughout his life, which will be awarded at the judgment seat of Christ (2 Cor 5:10).

Others take the position that the five crowns all refer to eternal life in heaven, which is awarded at the end of the age. If James has a specific reward in mind for the crown of life, it would be for people who have endured extreme trials and passed the test by remaining faithful to Jesus. They will receive the crown of life at the Judgment Seat of Christ.

God has promised this crown "to those who love him". Why have believers throughout the ages remained faithful to Christ in the midst of suffering, enduring persecution, and even facing martyrdom? The answer is because they love God! This is the incentive to remain faithful to him during afflictions. Jesus made it clear that the true disciple will express his love for Christ in a life of obedience (John 14:15, 24) regardless of the cost.

Insights and Application, (1:12)

Many people balk at the thought of serving God under the pretense of seeking rewards. Their objection is that we should serve God out of obedience because we love him, not because we are seeking rewards. However, there are many places in the Bible that inform us that God rewards us for our service to him. For instance, scripture tells us to lay up treasures in heaven, and that we will be rewarded for our service to God (Mat 6:20, 1 Tim 6:19, Col 3:24). Paul tells us we will be rewarded at the judgment seat of Christ (Rom 14:10, 2 Cor 5:10).

Parents use rewards to provide motivation and incentives to their children to promote acceptable behavior. God does the same thing with us—his children. He loves to bless and reward those who serve him. Therefore, looking forward to rewards can be a great source of incentive for believers to be faithful and obedient to God in the present. The thought of receiving rewards from the Lord serve as a motivational factor in enduring difficult times. Every believer longs to hear the Lord say, "Well done good and faithful servant" (Mat 25:21).

On one occasion Peter asked Jesus a question that is relevant to the discussion at hand. Read through the story of the rich young ruler located in Luke 18:18-30. Jesus told the rich man to go and sell everything, give the money to the poor, then come and follow me. Most commentators take the position that Jesus knew the man's attachment to his money was the very thing that was preventing him from becoming a devoted disciple. For that reason Jesus told him to give all his possessions to the poor, but the problem was he couldn't do it! His money and comfortable lifestyle were more important to him than following Jesus and receiving eternal life.

Commenting on the grip his money had on him Jesus said, "It is easier for a camel to go through the eye of a needle than for someone who is rich to enter the kingdom of God" (Luke 18:25). It made the people wonder how anybody can get saved, so Jesus made it clear that with God all things are possible (Luke 18:27).

A few verses later Peter weighed in on the discussion and made a comment that Jesus responded to in Luke 18:28-30:

> Peter said to him, "We have left all we had to follow you!" 29"Truly I tell you," Jesus said to them, "no one who has left home or wife or brothers or sisters or parents or children for the sake of the kingdom of God 30will fail to receive many times as much in this age, and in the age to come eternal life."

In essence Peter was asking Jesus, given the sacrifice we've made to follow you, what's in it for us? What do I get for being your disciple? Apparently, Jesus viewed Peter's question as valid, for he offered no rebuke to him. Jesus answered the question head on, to let the disciples know that there are great rewards in this life and the next, that accrue to believers for their sacrifices they make in following him. I would have loved to see the looks on the disciples' faces when Jesus said that. Did big smiles appear on their faces? Were they like deer staring in headlights? Did they not get it? One can only imagine the impact Jesus' words had on them.

Jesus' promise of blessing and reward for the disciple's sacrifice is a source of encouragement and incentive to continue on walking with the Lord. When we think about how great heaven will be, it should fill our hearts with hope for the future and provide us with incentive to keep on serving the Lord as we give him our best!

CHAPTER FIVE

"GOD ISN'T THE PROBLEM"

James 1:13-18

When tempted, no one should say, "God is tempting me." For God cannot be tempted by evil, nor does he tempt anyone; ¹⁴but each person is tempted when they are dragged away by their own evil desire and enticed. ¹⁵Then, after desire has conceived, it gives birth to sin; and sin, when it is full-grown, gives birth to death. ¹⁶Don't be deceived, my dear brothers and sisters. ¹⁷Every good and perfect gift is from above, coming down from the Father of the heavenly lights, who does not change like shifting shadows. ¹⁸He chose to give us birth through the word of truth, that we might be a kind of firstfruits of all he created.

Given the circumstances which led to James writing this homily, it is understandable how people could be upset with God for the hardships they were enduring. One way they fail a trial is by blaming their sinful behavior on God. Perhaps some of the believers were questioning God's goodness and His intentions with them, given the suffering they were enduring because of their faith in Christ.

Everyone faces temptations! Sometimes believers resist temptations and other times they cave into the sinful pressure. Rather than accepting responsibility for their actions people will often hold God responsible for their failures. Some people have a twisted theology and think that God has an axe to grind by deliberately tempting them to sin. James corrects this notion by presenting an accurate view of God, and places the responsibility for behavior squarely on each person's shoulders.

In the previous section we saw the proper way to go through a trial and pass the test of our faith. The trial is external to the believer referring to the circumstances that prevail in his life. This section deals with the internal aspect of dealing with circumstances that present themselves. Some people respond to trials improperly by giving into temptation and sinning. Then, they have the audacity to blame it on God!

When tempted, no one should say, "God is tempting me." For God cannot be tempted by evil, nor does he tempt anyone; (1:13)

The word "tempted" *(peirazo)* in v. 13, is a form of the same word translated "trial" *(peirasmos)* in vv. 2 and 12. The latter word is presented as a noun, whereas the former word is in the verbal form. The context makes it clear that v. 13 is referring to inner temptations to commit sinful behavior, whereas in vv. 2 and 12 the context indicates that trials consist of external circumstances. Thus, the word can have positive and negative connotations depending on the context.

When tempted to sin it is imperative to recognize the source of the temptation. It is not God! For God to tempt a believer to sin would be inconsistent with his character. God cannot be tempted by evil. The most enticing things that appeal to the human eye, stimulating our senses to commit sinful behavior, have no effect on God because of his moral perfection. God is immune to any evil influence because there is nothing in God that would appeal to anything sinful. God cannot be enticed by evil because of His holiness and moral perfection. It is even outside of the realm of possibility that God would be tempted or influenced in any way by evil.

Not only can God not be tempted by evil, "he doesn't tempt anyone". God does not influence people to sin. He has no evil intentions directed at his people to harm them spiritually, causing them to be shipwrecked regarding their faith. God allows temptation to come into believers' lives, but as temptations come God always gives us a way of resisting them through his grace (1 Cor 10:13). James is not saying that God never tests people. Clearly He does! For example, God tested the faith of Abraham and Job, but not with evil intentions to cause them spiritual disaster. James has just showed us the positive aspects of having our faith tested in trials (vv. 2-5), which God may deliberately do! However, this is entirely different than tempting one of his children to sin. This would mean that God has some evil intent with his people, which is not the case.

but each person is tempted when they are dragged away by their own evil desire and enticed. (1:14)

James places the source of temptations as being the person's own evil "desire" *(epithumia)*. This word is commonly translated lust, in either a good or bad sense depending on the context. Most of the time, the word carries sexual connotations with it in a negative sinful way. However, in the verse under consideration its meaning is broader than lust. Any desire that is inappropriate, that stands in stark contrast to the teaching of Scripture, is what James has in mind. The cause of the temptation is not God—it lies within each person. James is thinking about the innate capacity to sin, which exists in all people. The apostle Paul recognized this tendency to sin in his writings, calling it the sinful nature (Gal 5:16-17).

James is a creative thinker and comes up with colorful word pictures to illustrate his points. Such is the case here. The term dragged away (*exelko*) and enticed *(deleazo)* are terms used in hunting and fishing that describe a baited trap or hook, designed to lure the animal to it for its fatal capture. James sees temptation as the bait that attracts the sinner and captures him leading to his spiritual demise.

Then, after desire has conceived, it gives birth to sin; and sin, when it is full-grown, gives birth to death. (1:15)

James changes the metaphor from hunting and fishing to reproduction, and provides us with another colorful illustration to drive home his theology. Within each person evil desires linger that need to be resisted by depending on God. When desires within are entertained rather than resisted, sin is conceived. Once conceived the period of gestation takes place ending in giving birth to sin. When sin grows up and becomes dominant in a person's behavior it leads to spiritual death. James pictures the lifecycle of sin as running parallel to the lifecycle of a person from conception in the womb, gestation, birth, growth, and finally death.

Is James saying that when sin becomes habitual in a person's life that it leads to physical death, spiritual death, and ultimately eternal death? That presses the metaphor too far. The point James is making is that when sin becomes habitual in a person's life there are grave spiritual consequences to be faced. Sin results in separation from God, grieves the Holy

Spirit, and adversely effects the quality of one's walk with the Lord. When sin begins to reign over the sinner and make him the slave of sin, dire consequences exist for the believer (Ro 6:12-13). The Lord desires us to be freed from sinful habits, however, as Paul makes clear in Romans chapter six, the sin nature continues to be a force to be reckoned with throughout the life of the believer.

Experience indicates that Christians can fall into sinful patterns of behavior such as drug addiction, alcoholism, pornography, and so forth. The fact that these destructive sinful patterns of behavior exist doesn't mean they aren't truly born again believers, it indicates that their walk with the Lord isn't what it should be. They are Christians that are not utilizing their resources in Christ to overcome temptations. Sin can become full-grown in the sense that it dominates their lives (in certain areas) such that they are out of control and seem powerless to stop the behavior. They are still saved, however, they have much repenting to do, require ministry, prayer, Scripture reading, restoration, and so forth, to gain freedom.

James has shown his readers the right response to trials (vv. 2-5, 12) and the wrong response to trials (vv. 13-15), which are reflected in the columns below.

Right Response to Trials	Wrong Response to Trials
Testing of faith	Evil desire
Endurance	Temptation
Complete, lacking nothing	Sin is conceived
Approval of faith	Sin is born
Blessing – the crown of life	Sin becomes full grown
	Death results

This colorful illustration that James provides about the consequences of sin, should provide us with the incentive to watch our behavior! Sin can be lethal! It caused the fall of man resulting in physical death, spiritual death, it causes bondage to bad habits, and without Christ it leads to eternal death. God sent Jesus to redeem us from our sinful condition, so that we can walk in liberty now, and ultimately receive the crown of life, for those who place their trust in Him.

Don't be deceived, my dear brothers and sisters. ¹⁷Every good and perfect gift is from above, coming down from the Father of the heavenly lights, who does not change like shifting shadows. (1:16-17)

When a believer thinks that God is tempting him to sin and has evil intentions for him, this is evidence that the person is deceived. He has a twisted view of God that can have harmful consequences. It would be difficult to worship a God that you believe is out to get you! If your theology of God informs you that he is the tempter provoking you to sin, resulting in a damaged spiritual experience, how could you trust a god like that? It is Satan who is the Tempter not God! James is showing his pastor's heart to his audience by calling them "my dear brothers". He understands how under the duress of a trial people can get their perspective on God out of focus.

Entertaining this view of God indicates that the believer is deceived. He has basic theological errors in his view of God that need to be corrected, which is what James does in v. 17. The correct perspective of God is that He is the giver of every "good and perfect gift from above". God is the source of blessing in the believer's life, not the source of evil. God only gives good and perfect gifts. His gifts are not just OK, they good and perfect! His perfect gifts also include the trials that he brings into your life! This may be a hard pill to swallow, but it is true. What else could be expected from our heavenly Father, who is completely benevolent and morally perfect?

This passage brings to mind Jesus' description of God in the Sermon on the Mount: If you, then, though you are evil, know how to give good gifts to your children, how much more will your Father in heaven give good gifts to those who ask him (Matthew 7:11)!

Gifts from God come down from above from the "Father of heavenly lights". The word Father is not found in the Greek text, which means the translators of the NIV assumed that was the intended meaning of the author. This description of God indicates his sovereign role in the creation and maintenance of the universe. It is God who placed the stars and planets in the sky when he created the heavens and the earth (Gen 1:1). In the creation narratives in Genesis, it is clear that God's intention for the creation was to place man in a perfect world that consisted of everything that was good. Thus, the creation account is a reflection of God's moral goodness and benevolence that he directed toward man.

Like today, many in the ancient world were into astrology and paid attention to the stars, moon, and heavenly bodies. Throughout the day the shadows cast by the sun change as the earth rotates on its axis. Every month the moon goes through a cycle and appears in different forms; sometimes full, sometimes in an elliptical shape, and so forth. Throughout the year the formations of stars in the sky change as the earth rotates around the sun. Although there is constant movement and change with the heavenly bodies, God does not change like shifting shadows that are cast by the sun or moon.

God is the same yesterday, today and forever (Heb 13:8), the prophet Malachi informs us that the Lord does not change (3:6). God's moral goodness and benevolence is etched in cement—never to change. This is how the believer should view God. His goodness is a constant, and his love for us is like a cement platform that can't be moved.

He chose to give us birth through the word of truth, that we might be a kind of firstfruits of all he created. (1:18)

That God chose to give us the new birth (John 3:3 & 5), or regenerate the sinner (Titus 3:5), is evidence of his benevolence toward us, and is the greatest of all His gifts that a person can receive! The word of truth is the gospel message that if received by faith will result in the born again experience, and adoption into the family of God. For those who were questioning God's goodness and his intentions for them, they should be mindful of this great gift that God gave them, and how costly it was. Jesus had to die so that sin could be atoned for and we could be forgiven. That should eliminate any doubt about God's intentions for his people.

The reference to firstfruits was an agricultural term that points to the first part of the harvest, which was also an indication of what the rest of the harvest would look like. The Lord required that the firstfruits were to be offered to him, (Lev 23:10-11, Ex 23:19, Deu 18:4) rather than being stored in a facility in case the rest of the crop was lost to insects, drought, disease, or some natural disaster. The first part of the harvest was considered to be holy to the Lord; or set apart to God (Deu 18:4).

Calling the believers in the first Century "firstfruits" indicates that they were the first part of the initial gospel harvest, and are set apart to God. The church was in its infant stage, which made them the first believers to be harvested through the preaching of the "the word of truth" (the gospel). Paul referred to the believers in the household of Stephanas as the firstfruits in Achaia (1 Cor 16:15). Throughout the millennia there have been millions of people that have experienced the new birth through the preaching of the gospel. God is constantly creating and giving life! He did so in the initial creation account (v. 17) and continues to impart life spiritually as we are reborn, or recreated through faith in Christ. Thus, believers not only experience physical birth, but a spiritual rebirth when we receive Christ into our lives.

The new birth we receive should eliminate all thoughts entertained by believers that God has ill will toward us by tempting us to sin.

Insights and Application, (1:13-18)

Trials are a normal part of a believer's life. We all suffer hardships of various kinds, which can lead to an incorrect perspective of how God is working in our lives during these times. It is not uncommon for people under duress to say things like: "God why are you doing this to me?" "If you really care about me you wouldn't let this happen." "Since you are all powerful why don't you bring this trial to a screeching halt!" Under stressful situations we tend to get our perspective of God muddied, and begin to blame him for our problems. Isn't this what Adam and Eve did when they fell? The woman blamed it on the serpent, Adam blamed it on the woman and God, when he said to God "the woman you put here with me gave me some fruit and I ate it (Gen 3:12)." Adam had the audacity to blame God for his own failure!

One aspect of fallen humanity is that we tend pass the buck and not take responsibility for our actions. Such is the case with sin. We can get our view of God so warped that we think he is tempting us to sin, and has some hidden agenda to bring spiritual disaster upon us. We live in an age when biblical knowledge is at an all-time low, which is why people come up with such erroneous notions about God. This testifies to the fact that every believer needs to be grounded in a proper understanding of God's character.

It is interesting to note that James is writing to a group of biblically literate Jews who became Christians. Apparently, biblically literate folks can entertain false notions about God as well! One can have a great deal of biblical knowledge, but draw the wrong conclusions about God based on their circumstances. God is purely benevolent regarding his intentions toward us. When believers start viewing God like he is the Tempter, they are assigning to God the work of Satan. It is Satan who is described as the Tempter (Mat 4:3, 1 Thes 3:5) who has an agenda to trip up believers by influencing them to fall into sin.

The Bible places the responsibility for behavior squarely on each person's shoulders. When we stand before God on judgment day we are responsible for every thought, every word spoken, and every behavior committed. We have no justification for thinking we are freed of culpability for our actions. Excuses like: "the Devil made me do it", or "I just can't help it", or "the sinful nature is too strong", won't cut it on judgment day.

The modern-day believer has temptations abounding all around him. Sin looks great! If it didn't people wouldn't sin. There is a powerful lure that sin has. The metaphor that James used of people being dragged away and enticed by their evil desires (v. 14) provides a graphic picture of the power of sin. It is attractive, and it is deceptive. People take the bait, often knowing the spiritual damage that will result. The need for believers to be discerning is very apparent when studying a passage of this sort. Sin looks great, feels great, but afterwards the consequences can be devastating.

James used a metaphor of sin being parallel to the lifecycle of a human being (v. 15). When James says sin conceives, gives birth, becomes full-grown, then leads to death, we are reminded of the severity of sin. When sin becomes full grown, and a very bad habit is established in someone it can be devastating. People who are lured into the trap of drug or alcohol addiction will discover when that sin is full-grown in them they are virtually powerless to stop. The same can be said of gluttony, gambling, compulsive shopping, greed, pornography and so forth. It all looks so good, but once trapped by its seductive lure, one finds out they are under the control of that sinful tendency. It holds power over them and brings them to a sort of spiritual death, in the sense that sin separates us from God and makes us the slave to sin.

Ours is a society of addictions. Twelve step type programs exist in abundance, and are even taking on a Christian ambiance. One recent program out of Saddleback Church entitled "Celebrate Recovery" is a program designed to help people find freedom in Christ from a multitude of addictive behaviors. The best defense against getting trapped in sinful patterns of behavior is to avoid sin altogether, and obey God's word. When our evil desires begin to assert themselves within us, we need to utilize our resources in Christ to overcome the temptation! This is a part of spiritual warfare against the world, flesh, and the devil that many are missing today.

When believers wrongly assign the tempting work of Satan to God they are operating under a deception. People need to go through life understanding that God's intentions for them are wholly good. It would be difficult to place your trust in a God that has evil intentions with you. As believers come to understand that God is the source of only good and perfect gifts, this is a liberating thought that causes the believer to move toward God, not away from him. When the people of Israel left Egypt, beginning their trek in the desert, they grumbled at God by questioning his intentions for them, which stimulated the Lord's anger. The Israelites went through a prolonged trial as they wondered through the desert, thinking that God had it in for them, but nothing could be further from the truth.

All God's gifts are good and perfect (v. 17)! That means even the trials that come into our lives are to be viewed as gifts. If a trial comes into our life, then passes leaving a residue of holiness, spiritual stamina, and maturity, God is to be praised for such a work! God's character is constant—he never changes. He is always to be viewed as the giver of all that is good to his children. The believer needs to grasp this marvelous concept and live in that glorious truth!

The greatest gift God gives to sinners is the new birth (v. 18)! Whenever we start questioning God's goodness, we need to meditate on God's demonstration of love in sending Jesus to die on the cross on our behalf. Jesus was punished in our place, bearing the guilt of our sins so that we could be forgiven. All who receive Jesus into their hearts by faith are forgiven of their sins and are born again. All humanity is invited to come to Jesus by faith and receive eternal life. This should lay to rest any doubts about God's goodness!

CHAPTER SIX

"QUALITIES OF THE NEW BIRTH"

James 1:19-25

My dear brothers and sisters, take note of this: Everyone should be quick to listen, slow to speak and slow to become angry, [20]because human anger does not produce the righteousness that God desires. [21]Therefore, get rid of all moral filth and the evil that is so prevalent and humbly accept the word planted in you, which can save you. [22]Do not merely listen to the word, and so deceive yourselves. Do what it says. [23]Anyone who listens to the word but does not do what it says is like someone who looks at his face in a mirror [24]and, after looking at himself, goes away and immediately forgets what he looks like. [25]But whoever looks intently into the perfect law that gives freedom, and continues in it—not forgetting what they have heard, but doing it—they will be blessed in what they do.

The last section concluded with James backing up his statement that every good and perfect gift comes from God, by directing his readers' attention to the greatest of all gifts—the new birth! Once the new birth is experienced a radical transformation should occur in the new believer's life. What are the characteristics of the new birth? What changes should take place in the life of the new believer? As always, James is concerned with the practicality of the Christian life. It is to a discussion of the features of the new birth that we now turn.

Controlling our Anger, (1:19-20)

My dear brothers and sisters, take note of this: Everyone should be quick to listen, slow to speak and slow to become angry, [20]because human anger does not produce the righteousness that God desires.

By the repetition of "my dear brothers and sisters," James is including himself in his directives to his readers, while giving them a glimpse into his sensitive heart. The practicality of this passage is obvious, making it easy for the reader to track with what James is saying. Many times we speak before we think and end up putting our foot in our mouth, only to make us look foolish, and bring offense to others through our brash words. The remedy to this malady is simple but profoundly wise. Being "quick to listen and slow to speak" is great advice for the man who frequently gets himself in trouble—because he speaks before he thinks, and has a problem with anger. One who experiences the new birth has the quality of restraint. The wisdom literature in the Old Testament has much to say about the necessity of controlling one's speech. Below are a few passages that James may have drawn from in composing vv. 19-20:

> Sin is not ended by multiplying words, but the prudent hold their tongues. (Proverbs 10:19)

> A gentle answer turns away wrath, but a harsh word stirs up anger. (Proverbs 15:1)
>
> The one who has knowledge uses words with restraint, and whoever has understanding is even-tempered. [28]Even fools are thought wise if they keep silent, and discerning if they hold their tongues. (Proverbs 17:27-28)
>
> Do you see someone who speaks in haste? There is more hope for a fool than for them. (Proverbs 29:20)
>
> An angry person stirs up conflict, and a hot-tempered person commits many sins. (Proverbs 29:22)

Words spoken in haste can be hurtful, and once spoken cannot be retracted. The damage is already done! I once heard that for every negative comment directed at a person, it takes seven positive statements to undue the effect of the one negative remark.

One interpretation of being "quick to listen" refers to listening to the Word of God, while "slow to speak" refers to restraint in becoming teachers of the word. Being "slow to become angry" refers to the believer who is angry at God's Word for confronting his sinful behavior, or the person in question is angry because he outright disagrees with God's truth. This is, however, an unconvincing argument. It seems more likely that James is talking about exercising restraint in personal relationships by being good listeners, carefully selecting our words before we speak, and avoiding an angry response that only damages and possibly severs relationships. His emphasis is on human behavior!

In v. 20 James explains that mans' anger does not, in most cases, lead to the type of righteous life that God desires us to live. Certainly, there are times when righteous indignation is appropriate, as when Jesus drove out the money-changers from the Temple court yard (Mat 21:12, Jn 2:15). However, as a rule of thumb man's anger is usually contrary to the righteous standards God requires us to live by.

The one who has experienced the new birth and is growing in the word of God should be restrained in his responses to people. The word of God will serve as a guide to direct us down the path of the righteous life that God desires we live. When a believer becomes quick to listen, slow to speak, and slow to become angry (v. 19) he is showing evidence of a transformed life.

Getting Rid of Sin, Getting the Word in, (1:21)

Therefore, get rid of all moral filth and the evil that is so prevalent and humbly accept the word planted in you, which can save you. (1:21)

The word therefore, indicates that a conclusion is being drawn from the last verse, namely that we must "get rid of all moral filth and the evil that is so prevalent." The Greek word *(apotithemi)* comes into the NIV as "get rid" and is written in the Greek as a command. This word was commonly used of taking off clothing. Like taking off a dirty shirt, the believer is to get rid of all traces of the former life. Paul uses the word in a similar manner elsewhere (Eph 4:22, Col 3:8).

James commands his readers to get rid of all "moral filth", which translates the Greek word *rhuparia* which refers to any kind of defilement, or impurity. The word is used of Joshua (Zech 3:3-4) whose filthy clothes were replaced with new ones symbolizing the removal of sin from his life. The word therefore, refers to dirt, grimy filthy clothes, but spiritually refers to dirt that soils our souls. Moral filth residing in the life of a believer retards his growth as a disciple.

James also commands us to rid ourselves of the "evil that is so prevalent". The evil, *(kakia)* refers to malice, evil intentions, and ill will toward other people. James says this evil is prevalent or in excess and abundance. The believer is to get rid of these things and all traces of the former manner of life. This is done through confession, repentance, making deliberate choices to be obedient to God's word, and honoring the Lord.

Common sense indicates that if the believer is continuing to live a life governed by sin, the word of God will not have its intended effect. He will have difficulty hearing from the Lord, and letting the word have its impact on his life. After the disciple gets rid of his sinful behavior, he "humbly accepts the word planted in him". Therefore James is picturing the believer exchanging one thing for another: his sinful behavior is discarded and replaced with the word of God, which facilitates his growth in godliness.

"Humbly" is the translation of the word *prautes,* which denotes the idea of strength under control that enables one to accept the hardships that come into his life and remain even-tempered and stable.

The word is to be accepted, but not for initial salvation because that has already occurred. James is talking about letting the word of God do its work in the growth of the believer leading to maturity. If the Christian is walking in paths of sinful behavior, he is not receiving the word of God in such a way that it can change him and be a guiding light in his life. The word is "planted in you", which is a translation of *emphutos*; a word that denotes the idea of planting a seed in the ground. In this metaphor, James imagines the word of God being a seed that is planted in the heart of a believer and begins to take root and grow. One is mindful of the parable of the sower (Mat 13:3f) and the different types of soil representing the different conditions of the human heart. In that parable Jesus mentioned the "seed that fell on good soil is the man who hears the word and understands it. He produces a crop, yielding a hundred, sixty or thirty times what was sown (Mat 13:23)." This is the point James is trying to drive home! When the word of God goes into the right type of soil (heart) it will yield tremendous fruit in the believer.

It is important after being born again to keep our hearts open and receptive to the word of God, so that we don't impede our spiritual growth. James has told us to "humbly accept the word planted in you, which can save you". The way that the word can "save" us refers to what happens after regeneration occurs, which is the process of sanctification or growth in godliness. The word "save" is very broad in meaning. It can refer to the initial reception of Christ at conversion, the process of sanctification throughout the duration of the disciple's life, and our final glorification. James sees the word of God as the key ingredient that produces holiness in the life of a believer, and ultimately leads to our glorification when sanctification is completed.

Obeying God's Word, (1:22-25)

Do not merely listen to the word, and so deceive yourselves. Do what it says. [23]Anyone who listens to the word but does not do what it says is like someone who looks at his face in a mirror [24]and, after looking at himself, goes away and immediately forgets what he looks like. (1:22-24)

James has just told his readers to humbly accept the word implanted in you. If all we do is listen to the word, but don't obey God's word, we are not showing evidence of the new birth. In fact, without actively obeying the word we are deceiving ourselves. We are not dealing with spiritual reality. Professing to be a Christian and not obeying the word indicates that there is something drastically wrong with our spiritual performance. Studying Scripture isn't just to be done as an intellectual pursuit, or for entertainment, it is to be done for the purpose of doing what it says.

Jesus spoke of the importance of obeying the word when he said: "Therefore everyone who hears these words of mine and puts them into practice is like a wise man who built his house on the rock (Mat 7:24). The Lord indicated that doing what the word says is an expression of our love for him (John 14:15), making obedience one of the hallmarks of a disciple of Christ!

James provides us with another colorful illustration to give us further insight into the one who listens but doesn't obey the word. He is like a man who looks at his face in a mirror, then walks away immediately forgetting what he looks like. When we look at ourselves in the mirror we fix ourselves up! We comb our hair, ladies fix their makeup, and so forth. The point of contrast is the person who after listening to a sermon, or passage of scripture read aloud, walks away forgetting everything he has heard. The word had no effect on him.

Scripture is like a mirror in that it gives us a glimpse into ourselves. We may read a passage and be made aware that we excelled in doing what the passage taught. On the other hand, we may read a passage in the Bible that informs us of how disobedient we are, bringing us to the stark realization that we need to tighten things up spiritually! We read passages of God's word and are confronted with our shortcomings and sins that need to be repented of. After becoming aware of these things, we can't just close our Bibles, place them back on our desk, and walk away without making some changes. If that's what we do, we are the person James is describing: a man who listens to the word, but doesn't do what it says, and is deceived. This individual may think he is doing well in his spiritual experience, and making progress in studying the word of God, however his lack of obedience to Scripture testifies to his subpar performance. He is truly deceived.

But whoever looks intently into the perfect law that gives freedom, and continues in it—not forgetting what they have heard, but doing it—they will be blessed in what they do. (1:25)

James shifts gears from the man looking at himself in the mirror to the man who looks "intently into the perfect law that gives freedom". If he continues to look intently into the law and put it into practice, he will be blessed in his obedience. Unlike the man in vv. 23-24, who looks in the mirror and forgets, the man in v. 25 looks intently into the law, doesn't forget it, does what it says, and is thereby blessed!

The word translated *intently* is *parakypto* and portrays the idea of looking with a penetrating absorption, to lean over, or stoop down to ponder at something. It is the same word used to describe John stooping and peering into the tomb of Jesus (John 20:5). The point James is driving home is that studying Scripture requires more than just a quick look in the mirror (v. 24). Learning Scripture requires a close examination of each passage with a penetrating look that makes a lasting impression on the believer's heart! We don't read Scripture and then forget about it, we have the word of God in our heart to guide us (Ps 119:11).

What does James mean by the "perfect law that gives freedom"? Is this interchangeable with "the word of truth" mentioned in v.

18 and the "word" mentioned in vv. 21-23, or is there something else that James has in mind? Given the close association with "the word of truth", "word", and "perfect law" it seems that they all refer to the gospel, meaning essentially the same thing. In a purely Jewish sense, law refers to the Law of Moses and even the entire Old Testament. That James calls the law "the perfect law", casts the law into the shadow of what Christ did in fulfilling the law (Mat 5:17-18).

"The perfect law that gives freedom" points us to the new covenant promise that the prophet Jeremiah spoke of (31:31-34), particularly that it would be written on the minds and hearts of the worshipers. With the enabling power of the Holy Spirit, obedience to God's commands can be elevated to new heights. The author of Hebrews went to great lengths to describe the superiority of the new covenant over the old in chapters nine and ten, which should make the contemporary believer grateful that we live in the present age of fulfillment, which Jesus addressed in Matthew 5:17: "Do not think that I have come to abolish the Law or the Prophets; I have not come to abolish them but to fulfill them." Thus, James is describing the law from the perspective of Christ inaugurating the age of fulfillment through his death, resurrection, ascension, and sending of the Spirit.

One finds freedom from sin when obeying the "perfect law". Walking in God's ways keeps men and women free from the harmful consequences of sin. James has talked about how harmful sin can be when it becomes full grown (1:15) and leads to death. The overwhelming testimony of Scripture is that obedience leads to freedom. Consider the following passages:

> To the Jews who had believed him, Jesus said, "If you hold to my teaching, you are really my disciples. [32]Then you will know the truth, and the truth will set you free." (John 8:31-32)

> So if the Son sets you free, you will be free indeed. (John 8:36)

> Therefore, there is now no condemnation for those who are in Christ Jesus, ²because through Christ Jesus the law of the Spirit who gives life has set you free from the law of sin and death. (Romans 8:1-2)

> You, my brothers and sisters, were called to be free. But do not use your freedom to indulge the flesh; rather, serve one another humbly in love. (Galatians 5:13)

James ends v. 25 by stating that obedience to the word leads to blessing. It is precisely because obedience to the perfect law of God leads the worshiper to freedom from sinful behavior that one is blessed.

Insights and Application, (1:19-25)

People use the expression "born again" very loosely in our culture. Baseball players that break out of a batting slump and start knocking the ball out of the park, are often heard to say something to the effect of: "I feel like I'm born again!" Or when someone recovers from a long illness and regains their strength, will often comment on how they feel like they're born again. Of course the above usages of "born again" is a far cry from what the Biblical term means.

The result of accepting Jesus into one's heart through faith and repentance results in being born again. It is the entrance point into eternal life and the Kingdom of God (John 3:3 & 5). Once the new birth is experienced, the new believer should realize a transformation of his life, such that the qualities mentioned in the above passage are part of his existence. A true born again experience will result in a lifetime of following Jesus in obedience, serving him, and becoming more like him.

If I could pick a couple of verses that, if applied correctly, would enhance the quality of our lives, and the lives of the people around us, it would be vv. 19-20. James' practicality and simplicity is brilliant. The fruit of living out these verses will contribute greatly to having harmonious relationships, and make the world a kinder and gentler place.

The greater part of healthy communication is to be a good listener. James tells us to "be quick to listen". When the person you're talking too is distracted watching TV, or playing with their laptop, and not establishing eye contact with you it can be frustrating and insulting. If someone is hurting and they need your listening ear, but you're distracted they will pick up on that and feel slighted. They will feel devalued by you because you aren't paying attention to them, which can damage the relationship. The nonverbal message your poor listening skills will send the other person is: you're not important. Nonverbal communication, or your body language, is just as important, if not more important, than the words you speak.

Be an empathic listener. Empathy is the ability to step into someone's shoes and try to understand what they're telling you from their perspective. Try to feel what they're feeling. Try to connect with their joy or pain as you look at their nonverbal ques. Does their facial expression display sadness, happiness, anxiety, or anger? Is their body tense indicating they're amped up, energetic, or do they appear lifeless indicating they're sad and depressed? The good listener is dialed into the person they are conversing with by picking up on all their nonverbal communication. He puts down the remote to the TV, closes the laptop, establishes good eye contact, and listens empathically.

To show the person that you are listening intently, you can repeat back to him what he just told you. For example, at strategic points in a conversation you can say, "Let me see if I'm understanding you correctly. You're saying…" and then repeat back to him what he just told you. This listening technique informs him that you're listening, understanding, and are focused on him. Repeating back to the person what he's just told you will make him feel valued by you. If you didn't grasp what he said, repeating his words back to him gives him the chance to clarify anything that was misunderstood. The greater part of communication starts with listening, which is something we all need to work on.

James tells us to be "slow to speak" (v. 19). We've all spoken without thinking about the impact of our words, and we ended up putting our foot in our mouth by saying something hurtful and offensive. Once spoken, the words can't be retracted, and we usually feel pretty stupid after we blurted out our calloused words. What James is calling for here is a "measured response" to the people we are in dialogue with. In other words, pick your words carefully! Think before you speak! Consider if the words you choose will edify or hurt the person.

Being an empathic listener, should translate into being an empathic speaker. In other words, by stepping into the other person's shoes and understanding them because we are good listeners, will better equip us to respond in a meaningful way with our words.

The apostle Paul makes a significant contribution to our understanding of effective communication in Ephesians 4:29:

> Do not let any unwholesome talk come out of
> your mouths, but only what is helpful for building

others up according to their needs, that it may benefit those who listen.

If everybody could put this verse into practice, and eliminate all "trash talk" the world would be a much nicer place for everybody. The quality of your life and the lives of all whom you relate too would be greatly enhanced, if this verse of the Bible could be mastered! A simple rule of thumb to take from this verse is to speak what edifies the other person, and builds up the people who hear your words.

James says we should be "quick to listen, slow to speak and slow to become angry, because human anger does not produce the righteousness that God desires." (vv. 19b-20). Generally speaking an angry response to someone is a wrong response. There are times when righteous indignation is appropriate, such as when Jesus drove out the money changers from the Temple courtyard, but the vast majority of times man's angry response to others is sinful and contrary to the righteous life God desires. Therefore, it is better to have a "controlled response" to someone, rather than an "angry response". When the conversation becomes heated and we "loose it", the conversation ends with hurt feelings and a damaged relationship. This is contrary to what God desires. The best thing to do is stop the conversation before things get out of control.

The Word of God plays a crucial role in transforming believers, which is what James is emphasizing in vv. 21-25. Acquiring knowledge of Scripture isn't just an exercise in intellectual stimulation; it is for the purpose of putting into practice what the Bible says. In other words, we know the Bible has become part of us when we see our behavior transformed.

James drives home this point through his illustration of the word of God being a seed planted in the believer that grows and bears fruit (v. 21). Growing in our understanding of Scripture is crucial to growing in godliness. Biblical literacy is at an all time low in America today. Many children grow up never hearing about the basic Bible characters such as Moses, Joshua, King David slaying the giant, and so on. James makes it crystal clear that our growth as believers is tied to our reception of the word, such that every believer needs to be spending time studying Scripture.

James hits a grand slam with v. 22: "Do not merely listen to the word, and so deceive yourselves. Do what is says". At times all of us are guilty of making Scripture an intellectual exercise rather than a transformational reality. We may have attended a Bible study where the leader did a great job of driving home several points of Scripture, but during the week when numerous opportunities to apply what we just learned come into our life, we are oblivious to them. It was an interesting Bible study, but where's the application? Where is the obedience to God's word? What happened to life transformation? If all we do is acquire Biblical knowledge, but it doesn't transform our behavior, such that we are doers of the word, we are deceived in our spiritual experience. We may think that because we memorize Scripture and read the Bible often, that we are making great strides as a Christian, however, if we don't see the word of God changing our behavior such that we are a "Bible on display", we are deceived. We think we are growing mature disciples, when in actuality we are not. Disciples of Christ must read Scripture with a view to life transformation, not just intellectual stimulation.

We are blessed to be living in an age when so many resources are available to Christians. Commentaries on every book of the Bible are plentiful, numerous translations of the Bible exist, there are many study Bibles available, books on theology, and more, to help us grow in the Lord. Take the reading of Scripture as important as eating food every day.

CHAPTER SEVEN

"TRUE RELIGION"

James 1:26-27

Those who consider themselves religious and yet do not keep a tight rein on their tongues deceive themselves, and their religion is worthless. ²⁷Religion that God our Father accepts as pure and faultless is this: to look after orphans and widows in their distress and to keep oneself from being polluted by the world.

The word "religion" is a very spacious word that can mean just about anything these days. It can refer to a Buddhist, Hindu, Mormon, Christian, Spiritist, Baptist, Protestant, Catholic, and more. What do most people think about when they hear the term "religion", or are asked what it means to be a "religious person?" Perhaps, they think about keeping all the rules, being kind to people, being a person of high morals, and conducting themselves with ethical precision. They might regard religion as treating others the way they would want to be treated. James challenges his readers to reconsider what it means to be religious, in light of being born again. Being a religious person takes on a different dimension once someone enters the Kingdom of God.

Those who consider themselves religious and yet do not keep a tight rein on their tongues deceive themselves, and their religion is worthless. (1:26)

This section continues the discussion of the qualities of the new birth. One result of being born again is an altered perspective of how one views religion. James presents a person who considers himself to be "religious", which translates the Greek word *threskos*, which is found only here in the New Testament. The word pertains to outward acts of worship, and rituals, such as fasting, prayer, giving alms to the poor, and so forth. The point James is making is that true religion will be accompanied by ethical considerations such as controlling one's speech, looking after orphans and widows, and keeping oneself free from the polluting influences of the world.

From the Jewish perspective, there were a great many rites and rituals that were associated with the Temple sacrifices, festivals, and the whole corpus of Old Testament worship. Going through the motions of the rituals could be done with little or no heartfelt involvement, which was entirely offensive to God. This was precisely the point made in Psalm 50:8, where God is speaking to the Israelites and says, "I bring no charges against you concerning your sacrifices or concerning your burnt offerings, which are ever before me." God was not displeased with their sacrifices because they were supposed to present them. He was upset because they were doing them independently of any heartfelt devotion. Their actions had degenerated into an empty ritual that had become meaningless!

James has no place for religious practices that leave ethical matters behind. True religion is what happens when one experiences the new birth, and thus, lives a transformed life. Religion is a matter of the heart that must express love through good deeds, and lead to a holy lifestyle.

One quality of true religion is that the worshiper keeps a "tight reign on his tongue". "Tight reign" translates the Greek word *chalinagogeo*, which describes a bridle placed on a horse. It is as if the person under consideration has a run-away-mouth, like a horse running out of control. The person who worships God yet displays inappropriate language, whether it be gossip, slander, taking the Lord's name in vain, lying, unduly criticizing people, and so on, is deceiving himself. This man's religion is worthless, unacceptable to God! To experience the new birth and see no transformation in the area of one's communication indicates something is not as it should be in this person! If the individual with an out-of-control mouth thinks he is truly religious, he is operating under a self-delusion, and needs to check back into spiritual reality.

Religion that God our Father accepts as pure and faultless is this: to look after orphans and widows in their distress and to keep oneself from being polluted by the world. (1:27)

James gives us a picture of the type of religion that is acceptable to our God and Father. It must be "pure" (*katharos*) and "faultless" (*amiantos*), which are words used to describe moral purity. In other words, religion must not be ritualized acts, but deeds done with a heartfelt motivation to honor God by assisting those in need. Religion must have a practical application, which is what James envisions as God's people look out for "orphans and widows in their distress".

Perhaps, James identifies God as Father in this verse because he was mindful of Psalm 68:5, which identifies God as: "A father to the fatherless, a defender of widows, is God in his holy dwelling." God watches over orphans and widows in a special way and requires the same of his people (Ex 22:22, Deu 14:28-29, 27:19, Jer 7:5-7). The prophets God sent spoke harshly against the people of Israel because of their lack of compassion for the disenfranchised. A couple of examples are:

> "So I will come to put you on trial. I will be quick to testify against sorcerers, adulterers and perjurers, against those who defraud laborers of their wages, who oppress the widows and the fatherless, and deprive the foreigners among you of justice, but do not fear me," says the LORD Almighty. (Malachi 3:5)

> "Cursed is anyone who withholds justice from the foreigner, the fatherless or the widow." Then all the people shall say, "Amen!" (Deuteronomy 27:19)

Lacking in the social fabric of Israel was concern and compassion for those who couldn't defend themselves, and were easily neglected and abused. This was a grave sin in the eyes of God, because their display of justice was to be a reflection of God's justice and compassion. They failed miserably in this! James wants to see an expression of religion that surpasses that of Israel's defective religiosity.

Lastly, James says true religion translates into keeping oneself from being polluted by the world. Believers that succumb to the world's temptations can be spiritually soiled or stained. The world (*kosmos*) is the world system ordered independently of God, energized by Satan, and stands in stark contrast to God's ways and values. In other words, the world system is society that leaves God out of the picture, and places man as the final authority figure. Later in this homily James will rebuke his readers for having an adulterous relationship with the world (4:4), which is an appropriate admonition to the modern-day reader as well. The church is to be distinct from the world, but often times the two become indistinguishable from each other, because God's people are not expressing the true religion that is pleasing to God. James will have none of that!

Insights and Application, (1:26-27)

James has many things to say about our personal communication throughout his homily, which indicates that transformed communication is high on James' list of characteristics of the new birth. He's already told us that we should be quick to listen, and slow to speak (1:19). Things such as gossip, slander, lying, sarcasm, foul language, should disappear from the believer's vocabulary. If these things persist in a believer's life James would say his religion is worthless.

The term religion can mean just about anything in our culture. When you ask someone what religion they are you will hear a variety of answers such as: I'm Lutheran, I'm a protestant, I'm a practicing Catholic, I was raised as a Presbyterian, etc. However, none of these answers really indicate whether a person has received Christ into his life and been born again. Many people consider themselves religious, but don't have a clue about what it means to be born again.

Many individuals believe that being good, and helping other people through acts of mercy and kindness, are virtues to display, but they lack the new birth. As a pastor I'm always amazed at how many people grow up in church, only to be truly born again sometime later in their life. Before their born again experience, they may have thought they were religious, but didn't have a clue as to what the term born again meant.

My story is that I was raised Presbyterian, but didn't become a Christian until age 23. I didn't have a clue what the gospel was, but I would have considered myself a religious person, and if asked what religion I was I would have proudly responded Presbyterian! James challenges us to rethink what religion means. For many people religion is the ritual, going to church on Sunday, giving money to the Lord's work, being good people, and so on. For James true religion is accompanied by a heartfelt desire to show compassion and mercy to those in need such as orphans and widows. We might add to the list people in drug and alcohol rehab, prison ministry, highly dysfunctional people, the poor, illiterate, uneducated, handicapped, the sexually abused, and so forth. God expects us to show mercy to those who can't help themselves. Our actions, as God's people, are supposed to reflect his character. The manner in which the Christian community treats the hurting and disenfranchised of society, says a lot about the veracity of their walk with God.

I recently had a plumbing disaster in my home. Sewage backed up in my downstairs bathroom and came into the house. My plumber, who is a brother in Christ, commented that this was a messy job, not unlike the type of ministry that God has called him into. He explained that God called him to prison ministry, and he led the Celebrate Recovery ministry in his church. The type of people he works with are new Christians, many of which come out of a background of substance abuse, and are hurting people—pretty much regarded as the dregs of society. He said that doing ministry with those types of people is like the plumbing job he did for me, in that you get your hands dirty. Praise God for people like my plumber friend. True religion isn't just glamorous and convenient! Sadly, many Christians never step outside the protective walls of their church, and experience the blessing of rubbing shoulders with the dregs of society like Jesus did.

Finally, true religion requires keeping oneself free from the polluting influences of the world. The world offers a litany of temptations and many ways for a believer to plunge into spiritual disaster. True religion requires one to distinguish himself from the world, rather than blending into the world. The church has become worldly, making it increasingly difficult to separate the two. Many denominations ordain homosexuals, no longer believe the word of God is inerrant, question the efficacy of the cross, and are incredibly lenient toward sin.

It wasn't long ago that it came to my attention that one of the elders in a nearby church was a businessman, who owned a porn shop in town. What? You've got to be kidding! He was a long time member of the church and occupied a position on the board of elders for many years. This church has lost its ability to distinguish worldliness from godliness, and unfortunately has become polluted by the world!

Chapter Eight

"The Sin of Partiality"

James 2:1-13

My brothers and sisters, believers in our glorious Lord Jesus Christ must not show favoritism. 2Suppose a man comes into your meeting wearing a gold ring and fine clothes, and a poor man in filthy old clothes also comes in. 3If you show special attention to the man wearing fine clothes and say, "Here's a good seat for you," but say to the poor man, "You stand there" or "Sit on the floor by my feet," 4have you not discriminated among yourselves and become judges with evil thoughts?

Listen, my dear brothers and sisters: Has not God chosen those who are poor in the eyes of the world to be rich in faith and to inherit the kingdom he promised those who love him? 6But you have dishonored the poor. Is it not the rich who are exploiting you? Are they not the ones who are dragging you into court? 7Are they not the ones who are blaspheming the noble name of him to whom you belong?

If you really keep the royal law found in Scripture, "Love your neighbor as yourself," you are doing right. ⁹But if you show favoritism, you sin and are convicted by the law as lawbreakers. ¹⁰For whoever keeps the whole law and yet stumbles at just one point is guilty of breaking all of it. ¹¹For he who said, "You shall not commit adultery," also said, "You shall not murder." If you do not commit adultery but do commit murder, you have become a lawbreaker.

Speak and act as those who are going to be judged by the law that gives freedom, ¹³because judgment without mercy will be shown to anyone who has not been merciful. Mercy triumphs over judgment.

Ritualized religion that lacks any degree of compassion and mercy for the under-privileged people of society is unacceptable to James. The one who is born again will display a heart-felt sense of mercy and compassion for the poor, orphans, and widows while keeping himself free from the corrupting influences of the world. This is the kind of religion that James advocates because it expresses God's heart for the disenfranchised of society.

The partiality that James' readers were showing the rich nonbelievers at the expense of the poor believers indicates that their practice of religion wasn't what it should be. Given the length of this section, the sin of partiality must have been a serious problem for his readers. Scripture identifies God as being totally impartial in his dealings with us, so the church should follow in God's footsteps, reflecting that virtue in the way they deal with people. Their treatment of favoring the rich by giving them the seats of honor in the assembly was sinning against the poor believers. Even though they were being oppressed by rich people, rather than rebelling against them, they actually granted them special favors and privileges—how crazy is that! This favoritism toward the rich makes James' readers guilty of breaking the law, and lacking mercy in their relationships.

The Prohibition Against Favoritism, (2:1)

My brothers and sisters, believers in our glorious Lord Jesus Christ must not show favoritism. (2:1)

When a person places his faith in Jesus Christ he becomes a member of God's family. God adopts believers as his children (Ro 8:15-16) so believers become "brothers and sisters" in God's family. As such, showing any degree of favoritism is entirely inappropriate in the family of God, since God doesn't show favoritism in any way to his children. That God has accepted all people on the same criteria, namely their faith in Christ, indicates that God is totally impartial. He accepts all people the same way, showing no favoritism (Lev 19:15, Job 34:19, Pro 24:23, 28:21, Eph 6:9, Col 3:25, 1 Pet 1:17). He doesn't bend the rules and grant admission into the body of Christ because of external considerations, nor does he withhold discipline from anybody because of their social status. God gives equal treatment to all people, which is the standard for believers to emulate.

The phrase "Glorious Lord Jesus Christ" has glorious as an adjective modifying Lord Jesus Christ. In 1 Cor 2:8 Paul uses the term "Lord of glory," and in Acts 7:2 Stephen used the term "God of glory." The above uses of the term "glory" reflect the Hebrew word *kabod,* which means glory, or weight. One is reminded of the shekinah glory of God that settled upon the tabernacle in the desert, and filling the Temple at its dedication. In Jesus Christ we see the presence of God incarnate among us: "No one has ever seen God, but the one and only Son, who is himself God and is in closest relationship with the Father, has made him known (John 1:18)."

Glory could also be taken in apposition to Jesus Christ, which would render the phrase "The Lord Jesus Christ, the glory." Understood this way, "glory" is a name or title for Jesus. John said, "The Word became flesh and made his dwelling among us. We have seen his glory, the glory of the one and only Son, who came from the Father, full of grace and truth (John 1:14)." John makes it clear that Jesus is the glory of God the Father. To see Jesus is to see the glory of God, to see Jesus is to see the Father (John 14:9).

The phrase "show favoritism" is a translation of the Greek word *prosopolepsia*, which is literally "to receive face." The idea behind this phrase is making judgments about people based on external considerations such as looks, status, talent, money, intelligence, etc., and giving them preferential treatment based on these attributes. In our culture we often speak of the "face value" of something, which is similar to what James is referring to here.

An Example of Favoritism, (2:2-4)

Suppose a man comes into your meeting wearing a gold ring and fine clothes, and a poor man in filthy old clothes also comes in. ³If you show special attention to the man wearing fine clothes and say, "Here's a good seat for you," but say to the poor man, "You stand there" or "Sit on the floor by my feet," ⁴have you not discriminated among yourselves and become judges with evil thoughts? (2:2-4)

People are gathering for worship. As they come into the facility two people stand out of the crowd who are polar opposites. One man is wearing a gold ring and fine clothes, which reflects his status of wealth. In the Roman Empire clothing and jewelry were status symbols, so this man's appearance testifies to the fact that he is wealthy. The other man enters dressed in shabby clothes, which testifies to his poverty. The ushers give special treatment to the rich man and direct him to a good seat, but the poor man is offered the option of standing room only, or he can sit on the floor by the feet of the ushers. It was not uncommon in Jewish synagogues to offer seats of honor to those who gave money generously. They typically would be seated up in front closest to the pulpit.

James sees this as an unacceptable practice because they have "discriminated among themselves". They have given special treatment to the rich man solely on the basis of his looks, while slighting the poor man solely on the basis of his appearance. They don't have a clue what the spiritual life of either man is like! This violates the command of Leviticus 19:15: Do not pervert justice; do not show partiality to the poor or favoritism to the great, but judge your neighbor fairly.

They have "become judges with evil thoughts" in the sense that there may be ulterior motives behind their treatment of the rich man. Perhaps, they are thinking that a person of great influence will make a healthy donation when the offering is taken. Maybe they are thinking if they give him special treatment and wait on him hand over fist, that he will become a regular attendee, and they can count on his continued financial generosity, or other special favors!

God's Choice of the Poor, (2:5-7)

Listen, my dear brothers and sisters: Has not God chosen those who are poor in the eyes of the world to be rich in faith and to inherit the kingdom he promised those who love him? (2:5)

James calls them "brothers and sisters" for the second time in the passage (v. 1), which shows his tender heart, and that he is identifying with their situation. Most people in James' congregations were very poor. The irony of this statement is that James has to remind them that God has chosen them—the poor—to be rich in faith. They are dishonoring themselves (the poor) through their preferential treatment of the rich. It is as if they are acting against themselves. The role of one's status can't be underestimated in the culture of the Roman Empire. It was a culture based on the distinctions of privilege, pedigree, position, power, and of course, money. The poor believers that comprised the vast majority of James' audience were chosen by God for salvation. His choice of them is not to be understood as though He favors them over the rich, because that would make God guilty of the very sin of favoritism that James is speaking against in the community of believers. God doesn't love poor people more than he loves rich people!

James' point is that the world tends to marginalize, shun, and look down upon the poor and needy people of the world, but God doesn't! He is totally impartial and does not shun the poor and needy as the world does. He will look past a person's status and see a sinner that needs to be saved, whether she is rich or poor.

His readers have been elected by God to be rich in faith. In 1:10-11, James has discussed that in the kingdom perspective the rich (believers) occupy the low place, and the poor occupy a high place in the kingdom of God. The poor are the largest segment of the population in the Roman Empire, and the gospel spread attracting many of the impoverished people of the day. The poor are of no status in the eyes of the world, however, they occupy a special place in the eyes of God.

Although they are not rich in the material possessions the world has to offer, in Christ they are rich in faith! The poor Christians James is writing too are not distracted by materialistic concerns as the rich are, and focus themselves squarely on the riches of the gospel. Their richness of faith is seen in their daily dependence on their heavenly Father to supply them with all their needs, while he sustains them through the hardships they were enduring. The rich don't need to depend on God for their daily provision, because of their secure financial position.

God also chose the poor "to inherit the kingdom he promised to those who love him". Entering the Kingdom is synonymous with being born again (John 3:3, & 5). When we receive Jesus into our hearts by faith we enter the Kingdom of God, which is the place where Jesus reigns. We do not experience the Kingdom of God in its fullness at this time, however, Scripture teaches that this age will come to conclusion and the Kingdom of God will be revealed more fully in the next age (1 Thess 1:10, 1 Tim 6:19). Believers are said to be in a position where in the future they will realize their inheritance. The Lord Jesus and the apostle Peter made mention of the inheritance that awaits God's people:

> "Then the King will say to those on his right, 'Come, you who are blessed by my Father; take your inheritance, the kingdom prepared for you since the creation of the world." (Matthew 25:34)

> Praise be to the God and Father of our Lord Jesus Christ! In his great mercy he has given us new birth into a living hope through the resurrection of Jesus Christ from the dead, 4and into an inheritance that can never perish, spoil or fade. This inheritance is kept in heaven for you, (1 Peter 1:3-4).

Although the poor don't experience the lifestyles of the rich and famous in this life, they have a glorious inheritance to look forward to in the future, which fills them with hope. The inheritance promised to believers is not based on one's poverty it is specifically for "those who love him" (v. 5). Whether one is rich or poor, love for the Lord is expressed by receiving Jesus into your heart, thus qualifying the believer to gain admission into the Kingdom of God.

But you have dishonored the poor. Is it not the rich who are exploiting you? Are they not the ones who are dragging you into court?, (2:6)

By extending preferential treatment to the rich nonbelievers, the poor disciples were insulting their own kind! Perhaps, they were thinking that by giving special favors to the rich, favors might be returned, such as hefty donations, job offers, protection, and so forth. In light of the fact that the rich were exploiting poor believers by utilizing the court system to take legal action against them, makes the special treatment of the rich even more reprehensible!

Most likely, James is referring to rich land owners, who were exploiting the poor by using the courts to swindle land from them, which made them richer, while those who were already underprivileged lost everything! To make matters even worse, the rich would often hire the ones they exploited as day laborers to work the land they had taken out from under their feet! The special treatment of the rich was driven by sinful motives that were only adding insult to injury to their fellow poor brothers in the Lord.

Are they not the ones who are blaspheming the noble name of him to whom you belong? (2:7)

Another infraction of the rich against the poor believers was that they are blaspheming the name of Christ. In what manner were they doing this? It could be that they were speaking against Jesus in a disrespectful manner, mocking his divine status, while taking his name in vain much like people do today. Additionally, it could be that they were persecuting the poor not just economically through the courts, but by heaping verbal abuse on the Christians. They may have been harshly criticizing them for their beliefs, making fun of them, and mocking them, which is not uncommon for believers to experience in any age!

Because believers are united with Christ, when someone blasphemes the name of Christ, it indirectly comes upon his disciples. We have the name of Christ conferred upon us when we become a believer, and are baptized in the name of the Son (Mat 28:19). Scripture informs us that the disciples were first identified by Christ's name, by being called Christians at Antioch (Acts 11:26). What an honor to be identified as Christians, bearing the Savior's name! Too think that those who blaspheme the name of Christ were given special treatment within the church, points to the folly of such activity.

Favoritism Violates The Royal Law, (2:8-11)

If you really keep the royal law found in Scripture, "Love your neighbor as yourself," you are doing right. (2:8)

The royal law is the kingdom law, which originated with Jesus. This indicates that James was familiar with the teaching of Jesus that he left behind him (Mat 22:36-40). "Love your neighbor as yourself" is a quote from Leviticus 19:18. Favoritism violates this principle, which according to Jesus is the second greatest command in all of Scripture. Favoritism is contrary to extending love to your neighbor. Of interest is the fact that Jesus took the Shema, (Deu 6:4-5) which every Jew recited twice per day, and added to it "Love your neighbor as yourself (Lev 19:18), as recorded in Matthew's gospel:

> "Teacher, which is the greatest commandment in the Law?" [37]Jesus replied: "'Love the Lord your God with all your heart and with all your soul and with all your mind.' [38]This is the first and greatest commandment. [39]And the second is like it: 'Love your neighbor as yourself.' [40]All the Law and the Prophets hang on these two commandments." (Matthew 22:36-40)

The first and second commands are linked together, because if one is loving God correctly, he will be quick to extend that same love to his neighbor. Love for God and man can't be separated (1 John 2:9-11, 4:21). Where love is present, favoritism will be absent! James indicates to his readers that if they eliminate favoritism and properly love their neighbor they are doing right.

But if you show favoritism, you sin and are convicted by the law as lawbreakers. [10]For whoever keeps the whole law and yet stumbles at just one point is guilty of breaking all of it. (2:9-10)

The rabbis debated over which were the "lighter" versus "heavier" commandments found in the law. A tendency may have existed to excuse violations of the "lighter" commandments of the law, while enforcing the "heavier" commandments. Some may have felt showing favoritism was violating one of the lighter commands and therefore wasn't that big of a deal! James would disagree and respond with a firm "that's unacceptable"!

Not only does extending favoritism make one guilty of sinning, that infraction makes the culprit guilty of being a lawbreaker. The law serves as the judge and jury, and convicts the person of being a lawbreaker. For the Jews, keeping the law was of paramount importance. Nobody wanted to be guilty of being a lawbreaker. There can be no gradients of sin such that there are lesser sins that are permissible, and greater sins which are unacceptable. The sin of favoritism makes one a lawbreaker because the law is a whole unit (v. 10). If you can keep the entire law meticulously, yet break just one part of it, you have broken the law in its entirety. Why? Because the law is a unit—a complete whole that can't be separated. Jesus (Mat 5:18-19, 23:23) and Paul (Gal 5:3) both affirm the unity of the law in their writings.

For he who said, "You shall not commit adultery," also said, "You shall not murder." If you do not commit adultery but do commit murder, you have become a lawbreaker. (2:11)

By citing adultery and murder, which are certainly considered "heavier" commandments to be obeyed at all costs, James is indicating the sin of favoritism is just as serious as those are. Rather than marginalizing the sin of favoritism, it should be regarded as serious as the sin of adultery and murder. In no way can the sin of favoritism be justified because someone is keeping the 10 commandments—the weightier things of the law. That doesn't cut it with James!

Speak and act as those who are going to be judged by the law that gives freedom, ¹³because judgment without

mercy will be shown to anyone who has not been merciful. Mercy triumphs over judgment. (2:12-13)

Speaking and acting covers all human behavior. People should be mindful that on judgment day they have to give an account of their actions, and their judge will be the revealed will of God—the Scriptures. James has thus far identified the law as the royal law (2:8), now he identifies the law as that which gives freedom (v. 12). One might think that adherence to the law would be painfully burdensome and oppressive. However, one characteristic of God's law is that compliance to it produces freedom (John 8:31-32), not bondage. God's commands are not burdensome, and our consideration of the law must be viewed from our vantage point as New Testament believers—Jesus fulfilled the law (Mat 5:17). Obeying God's word brings the disciple of Christ to a place of freedom from sin and its harmful effects, such that he can enjoy the abundant life the Lord Jesus offers.

The freedom given by the law isn't to be interpreted as a license to sin. Rather, our freedom should enable us to serve one another in love, and more effectively serve the Lord. The law that gives freedom should lead the disciple of Christ to renounce sinful ways and live a godly lifestyle. The following passages describe how freedom should result from obeying God's word:

> You, my brothers and sisters, were called to be free. But do not use your freedom to indulge the flesh; rather, serve one another humbly in love. [14]For the entire law is fulfilled in keeping this one command: "Love your neighbor as yourself." (Galatians 5:13-14)

> Live as free people, but do not use your freedom
> as a cover-up for evil; live as God's slaves. (1
> Peter 2:16)

Understood from the perspective of New Testament believers, the law is not a series of oppressive legalistic codes. James is using Old Testament language because he is addressing Jewish Christians, so he is talking their language when he mentions the law, which is near and dear to the heart of any Jew. The apostle Paul often spoke of the law in terms that stand in stark contrast to that of James. Paul spoke of the law making one a slave to sin as if the law was an oppressive force to be contended with, not a code that if obeyed led to freedom as James describes. For example, Paul said in Romans 7:5-6:

> For when we were in the realm of the flesh, the
> sinful passions aroused by the law were at work
> in us, so that we bore fruit for death. ⁶But now,
> by dying to what once bound us, we have been
> released from the law so that we serve in the
> new way of the Spirit, and not in the old way of
> the written code.

Paul's emphasis on the law differs from James in that he was emphasizing the law as something we need to be freed from, so we can walk in the Spirit. In Paul's theology of the Spirit, the believer who walks in the power of the Holy Spirit will never violate the intent of the law. James was emphasizing the freedom that comes from obedience to the law, which Paul certainly would agree with. Even though James uses very Jewish language because of his audience, he would be in agreement with Paul that the law is fulfilled in Christ.

Both James and Paul would agree that walking in obedience to God's word (law) has a liberating effect upon the believer, and is the pathway to experiencing the abundant life Christ has to offer. When James speaks of the law he is doing so as it is fulfilled by the death and resurrection of Christ. He is speaking about the law in a similar way as Jesus did when the Lord said, "Do not think that I have come to abolish the law or the Prophets; I have not come to abolish them but to fulfill them (Mat 5:17)."

As the believer considers the future judgment awaiting him, he should be mindful of the criteria of the judgment. Christians will be judged by the Law that gives freedom (v. 12), the royal law (2:8), and the principle of mercy (vv. 12-13). If we do not show mercy to others we cannot expect God to show us mercy on judgment day. James' readers must realize that showing favoritism to the rich, at the expense of the poor, is contrary to displaying mercy. Since God has displayed mercy to all who believe in Christ, and thus do not receive eternal punishment as deserved, the principle of mercy should govern disciples' treatment of other people. When we fail to live as God instructs us, we always have his mercy to fall back on! Praise God! As those who have received such rich mercy from above, how can we withhold mercy from others!

Those who show no mercy to others have probably not been born again and will receive judgment without mercy. On the other hand, those who walk in mercy and extend it to others display the very character of God in their lives, not showing favoritism—the sin under consideration.

James concludes this section with "mercy triumphs over judgment." The mercy we show to others testifies to our saving faith, which will triumph over God's judgment of us on the day we stand before him. Those who have received God's mercy through Christ must be mindful that mercy should be a defining characteristic of their lives, which ensures their triumph over God's judgment. Displaying favoritism to the rich, at the expense of the poor, is a violation of the mercy ethic that should be characteristic of any born again believer.

Insights and Application, (2:1-13)

This passage of Scripture has numerous applications. Being totally fair and impartial isn't easy! Coaches have their favorite players, parents have their favorite child, teachers have their favorite students, and bosses have their favorite employees. We all struggle with being totally fair and impartial, however, the Lord doesn't. How comforting it is to know that he treats all his people equally, on a level playing field, so we don't need to feel like we're the odd man out with God! We don't need to feel like second class citizens in God's Kingdom, as if he favors others over us.

We often make distinctions about people based on nothing but externals. People in the Chicago area where I live are very diverse. Go into a local grocery store and you will see Asians, East Indians, African Americans, Hispanics, Caucasians and more. In a city like Chicago with all the diversity that exists, we can either dislike anybody that is different than we are, or learn to appreciate the richness of God's diversity.

When judgments are made about people solely on the basis of external considerations, and this is taken to an extreme, very bad things can happen! One only needs to remember a very dark period of history, the holocaust where six million Jews were systematically eliminated. This occurred because one group of people made prejudicial discriminations against people of other nationalities, races, religions, and so forth. Anybody that wasn't just like the Nazis was either enslaved or exterminated! There was no tolerance for people that were different than they were.

I remember shortly after becoming a Christian I began attending a singles Bible study in a mega church. On one occasion I met this guy who rubbed me the wrong way! He had a tie-died T-shirt on, with long wavy hair, and a scruffy looking pair of blue jeans with holes in various places. My God, he was a hippie! I'd have none of that because I was a jock, and jocks and hippies don't mix well! I just didn't like the man, but I had nothing to base that conclusion on because I didn't even know him.

My attitudes toward him were completely based on his appearance, taking into consideration nothing about what was in the man's heart. After I got to know him and heard some of his comments in Bible discussions, I began to see that he had some real spiritual depth—much more than I had. After more conversations, and encounters with him, I began to see that he wasn't such a bad guy after all! My initial impression of him was clouded by my prejudicial attitudes about hippies, which prevented me from looking at him like he was a human being, no different than I.

As a pastor, I need to make sure that I am fair and impartial in dealing with people to the best of my ability—it's not easy! I need to be cautious not to warm-up to those who are making the greatest financial contributions to the church, while shying away from those who give sparingly. Christians can at times be some of the most unforgiving people on the planet. For example, the single mom who just went through a rough divorce might get a cold shoulder from her friends at church, as if she is now a second class citizen in the Kingdom of God. The guy who's out of work and keeps draining the benevolence fund may come to be viewed as a nuisance, rather than a dear brother in Christ. The Christians who suffer from depression and take medication may have other believers call their faith into question, as if they're a sub-par Christian with the root of their depression being that they're not trusting Jesus! We all tend to make judgments based on external factors like the above, and discriminate against each other, which is not acting in love. This passage should serve as a check against jumping to prejudicial conclusions about people we worship with!

In verses 8-11 James pointed out for his readers that the law is a unit, thus, if you break one part of the law you are a lawbreaker. Rabbis of the day tended to distinguish between lighter and weightier commandments, as if it was OK to break the lighter commands, but unacceptable to break the weightier ones. All attempts to justify any sinful behavior, no matter how flagrant or miniscule the sin, are unacceptable! We've all heard the full gamut of excuses: everybody else does it! It doesn't hurt anybody! It's not as bad as you think! God understands! It's genetic I can't help it! The Devil made me do it! The Christian response to sin is confession and repentance, not justification. When we show favoritism to someone at the expense of another, we can't justify it by saying something like, "It's no big deal, it's not like I murdered somebody!"

In the Christian community we must display mercy to one another (vv. 12-13). All believers will one day face the Lord on judgment day. The criteria of the judgment will be the believer's adherence to the revealed will of God; or as James says the law that gives freedom. Whenever I meditate on the Biblical teaching on judgment day, it has a sobering effect on me. It makes me take the way I live my life very seriously, for I have to answer to God for everything I do! One specific criterion of God's evaluation of my life regards the way I showed mercy to others.

Since God has been merciful to me, I need to respond in like fashion to others! How can I receive God's mercy yet extend none to the people in my life, especially those who have wronged me! After all, I have wronged God many times. God may say to me I've been merciful to you, why haven't you been merciful to others. My display of mercy triumphs over God's judgment of me. Mercy should be a characteristic of any disciple's life, thus proving that he is truly born-again.

Chapter Nine

"What is True Saving Faith"?

James 2:14-26

What good is it, my brothers and sisters, if someone claims to have faith but has no deeds? Can such faith save them? [15]Suppose a brother or a sister is without clothes and daily food. [16]If one of you says to them, "Go in peace; keep warm and well fed," but does nothing about their physical needs, what good is it? [17]In the same way, faith by itself, if it is not accompanied by action, is dead. [18]But someone will say, "You have faith; I have deeds." Show me your faith without deeds, and I will show you my faith by my deeds. [19]You believe that there is one God. Good! Even the demons believe that—and shudder.

You foolish person, do you want evidence that faith without deeds is useless? [21]Was not our father Abraham considered righteous for what he did when he offered his son Isaac on the altar? [22]You see that his faith and his actions were working together, and his faith was made complete by what he did. [23]And the scripture was fulfilled

that says, "Abraham believed God, and it was credited to him as righteousness," and he was called God's friend. ²⁴You see that a person is considered righteous by what they do and not by faith alone.

In the same way, was not even Rahab the prostitute considered righteous for what she did when she gave lodging to the spies and sent them off in a different direction? ²⁶As the body without the spirit is dead, so faith without deeds is dead.

Authentic Christianity begins with authentic faith! James directs his readers to a picture of what true saving faith looks like. The born again Christian will live a life that is characterized by good works, such as showing mercy (v. 13), that stem from his vital faith in Christ. Many people see tension, and sometimes even a contradiction, between Paul and James regarding the doctrine of justification by faith alone. Paul's emphasis is that the believer is justified solely on the basis of faith, apart from any human performance of good deeds (Ro 5:1). James' emphasis focuses on the results of justification by faith; namely a lifestyle of good works. Once justified by faith, good works will be evident in the convert's life. Good deeds are a characteristic of those who possess real saving faith. The two, saving faith and good works are inseparably linked together!

It is interesting to note that James concluded the previous section by speaking of God's judgment. One with faith that produces no good works will not stand up under the scrutiny of the Almighty's judgment!

The Question About Saving Faith, (2:14)

What good is it, my brothers and sisters, if someone claims to have faith but has no deeds? Can such faith save them? (2:14)

James poses two questions to his audience regarding the nature of true saving faith. The first question asks "what good it is to claim having faith but no good works"? The answer is that it is worthless and pays no dividends to its owner whatsoever. The second question is "can such faith save him"? The Greek construction expects the no answer. Faith that produces no good works has no efficacy to save the person in possession of that type of faith. True saving faith will result in a lifestyle of good works. If there are no good deeds present in a person's life, his faith is worthless, and it can't save him.

An Example of Dead Faith, (2:15-17)

Suppose a brother or a sister is without clothes and daily food. ¹⁶If one of you says to them, "Go in peace; keep warm and well fed," but does nothing about their physical needs, what good is it? (2:15-16)

This is a hypothetical situation, but one that was probably somewhat common given the circumstances his readers were facing. They were enduring harsh economic times and many people were just barely getting by. When a fellow brother or sister (meaning a fellow Christian) comes across your path with obvious physical needs, we are obligated to help him out, especially if we have the means available to us. By wishing him well and "blowing him off" this person testifies to his superficial faith and his hypocrisy! True saving faith will move one to reach out to the needy and lend whatever assistance they can. Doing nothing to alleviate their physical needs serves no benefit to the one in need, or to the one who could potentially help the distressed individual out.

The apostle John said something similar to James: "If anyone has material possessions and sees his brother in need but has no pity on him, how can the love of God be in him (1 John 3:17)?" John sees the unwillingness of the person to lend assistance as a problem of the heart. Where's the love of God! James, on the other hand, sees the unwillingness of the person to render help being a problem of faith. Either way, true saving faith propels the person to action, causing him to lend a helping hand to those who are distressed.

In the same way, faith by itself, if it is not accompanied by action, is dead. (2:17)

The words spoken above to the needy person (2:16) don't cut it with God! True faith will lend itself to action, not empty words of insincerity. Pronouncing a blessing, saying prayers for the hurting, wishing someone well without taking any action, indicates that person's faith is sterile. If true saving faith was in the speaker (2:16), mercy would have kicked in and led the man to action. The fact that it didn't indicates that his faith is dead, incapable of saving him.

Proving Your Faith, (2:18)

But someone will say, "You have faith; I have deeds." Show me your faith without deeds, and I will show you my faith by my deeds. (2:18)

James shows us the futility of trying to separate faith from works, as if they are two distinct qualities, existing independently of each other. Faith and works are two links in a chain that can't be separated, as if one believer can just have faith, and the other can just have deeds. James asks the one who has faith to "show me your faith without deeds." In other words, James is saying prove you have faith; back it up! Put your money where your mouth is! Without works to support the man's profession of faith, he can't prove his faith in Jesus is genuine! He can boast about his faith all day, but in the absence of any works he can't prove his faith is real. The burden of proof will not be lifted from his shoulders until he can produce good works!

On the other hand, the one whose lifestyle consists of good deeds is showing everyone his faith is genuine by the good works he is doing. This believer can back up his profession of faith, because his lifestyle of good works bears witness to the profession of faith in Christ. The point James is making is that faith and works go hand-in-hand and are inseparable.

Faith Isn't Just Correct Theology, (2:19)

You believe that there is one God. Good! Even the demons believe that—and shudder. (2:19)

James is going to give us three examples of saving faith. The first (v. 19) is a negative example regarding the faith of demons, which is followed by two positive examples of faith from the patriarch Abraham, then the prostitute Rahab.

Another characteristic of authentic saving faith is that it involves more than a comprehension of correct doctrine, confessional statements, creeds, Scripture memory, and so forth. The belief that there is one God (monotheism) is central to Judaism and Christianity. Having a congregation that believes the essential doctrines of the Bible, and has a grasp of theology would make any pastor proud of his flock. James says this is good! However, the demons believe in monotheism and that doesn't do them much good! The demonic realm, and Satan himself, understands the doctrines of the Bible, and theology better than most of God's people, but they obviously don't have saving faith. They believe in God but shudder in fear, rather than bowing to the Lord Jesus in worship and obedience.

Of course, Jesus didn't die to redeem fallen angels he died to redeem mankind. There is no evidence in Scripture that suggests the fallen condition of angels is reversible through faith in Christ. Once the angels fell from their position of grace through their rebellion, they remain where they are in an unredeemable place for all eternity.

The Example of Abraham's Faith, (2:20-24)

You foolish person, do you want evidence that faith without deeds is useless? [21]Was not our father Abraham considered righteous for what he did when he offered his son Isaac on the altar? [22]You see that his faith and his actions were working together, and his faith was made complete by what he did. [23]And the scripture was fulfilled that says, "Abraham believed God, and it was credited to him as righteousness," and he was called God's friend. [24]You see that a person is considered righteous by what they do and not by faith alone. (2:20-24)

Knowledge of God and faith in him, like that of demons, doesn't lead to God's acceptance of the sinner. Faith in Jesus that produces good works is the type of faith that leads to one's acceptance by God. James provides an illustration for his readers from the life of the patriarch Abraham, to demonstrate that faith without works is useless. By saying "you foolish man" he implies that everybody should know this, as if it should be common knowledge.

One of the greatest Bible stories is found in Genesis 22, where God tested Abraham by telling him to sacrifice his son Isaac, at Mount Moriah. The patriarch obeyed the Lord by placing his son on the altar, and with knife in hand was ready to slay Isaac, until a divine intervention occurred:

> But the angel of the LORD called out to him from heaven, "Abraham! Abraham!" "Here I am," he replied. ¹²"Do not lay a hand on the boy," he said. "Do not do anything to him. Now I know that you fear God, because you have not withheld from me your son, your only son." ¹³Abraham looked up and there in a thicket he saw a ram caught by its horns. He went over and took the ram and sacrificed it as a burnt offering instead of his son. ¹⁴So Abraham called that place The LORD Will Provide. And to this day it is said, "On the mountain of the LORD it will be provided." ¹⁵The angel of the LORD called to Abraham from heaven a second time ¹⁶and said, "I swear by myself, declares the LORD, that because you have done this and have not withheld your son, your only son, ¹⁷I will surely bless you and make your descendants as numerous as the stars in the sky and as the sand on the seashore. Your descendants will take possession of the cities of their enemies, ¹⁸and through your offspring all nations on earth will be blessed, because you have obeyed me." (Genesis 22:11-18)

In response to Abraham's act of obedience the angel of the Lord said: "Now I know that you fear God, because you have not withheld from me your son, your only son (Gen 22:12)." How was it that the angel of the Lord knew Abraham feared God? It was through an act of radical obedience! His faith was

103

confirmed by his actions. According to James, Abraham was considered righteous for doing this. His faith and actions were inseparably working together, and his faith was made complete by his act of obedience (2:22). The Greek word *teleioo* is translated complete, but it also has the meaning of being made perfect, to mature, to accomplish a goal, or bring to an end. Thus, when Abraham committed this act of radical obedience, his faith was brought to completion! He accomplished the goal of faith, which is obedience—in this case radical obedience! Abraham's faith was made complete by being obedient to the Lord, which caused his faith to soar to new heights of maturity and vibrancy.

Abraham's act of obedience fulfilled the Scripture, which says "Abram believed the LORD, and he credited it to him as righteousness (Gen 15:6)." This appears to be the moment that Abraham placed his faith in God and the Lord conferred a righteous status upon him. Years later, when Abraham obeyed the Lord (through the Isaac episode) it verified and gave deeper meaning to the initial moment Abraham came to faith in God, and received the righteous declaration from the Lord. Every act of obedience fulfills a believer's initial conversion experience, where he is justified and has Christ's righteousness imputed to him. Radical acts of obedience are a bold proclamation that a believer's conversion was real! That is the sense in which our obedience "fulfills" our initial justification by faith.

The apostle Paul quotes Genesis 15:6 in Romans 4:23-24 where he says:

> The words "it was credited to him" were written not for him alone, [24]but also for us, to whom God will credit righteousness—for us who believe in him who raised Jesus our Lord from the dead.

This is critical to Paul's understanding that justification is by faith alone, and justification is always accompanied by the imputation of Christ's righteousness to the sinner, such that he is in a right standing with the Lord. However, Paul would be in agreement with James that once justified, the believer should live a lifestyle that consists of a vibrant faith that works itself out in radical acts of obedience.

The moment of Abraham's belief was also the time when his relationship with God was redefined. Now Abraham is "called God's friend". In Judaism Abraham is known as the exemplary friend of God. This is not a direct quote from Scripture but a paraphrase of either Isaiah 41:8, or 2 Chronicles 20:7, where Abraham is referred to as "the one loved by God." In addition to God's declaration of righteousness conferred upon Abraham because of his faith, he enjoyed a new level of intimacy with God. Jesus told his disciples in the Upper Room Discourse:

> You are my friends if you do what I command. [15]I no longer call you servants, because a servant does not know his master's business. Instead, I have called you friends, for everything that I learned from my Father I have made known to you. (John 15:14-15)

The pathway to friendship with the Lord Jesus was obedience. The deeper one goes in faith that expresses itself in works, will result in a proportionate level of intimacy with the Lord!

James brings us to his conclusion: "You see that a person is considered righteous by what they do and not by faith alone (v. 24)." This is another way of saying that the sinner who is considered righteous (justified) will have a faith that translates into bold works. The believer's works are the proof of his righteous standing with God. The true believer has a faith that can't be suppressed, shackled, or silenced! Living faith bursts forth and expresses itself in obedience. This is the sense in which James says a believer is considered righteous by what he does and not by faith alone.

The Example of Rahab's Faith, (2:25)

In the same way, was not even Rahab the prostitute considered righteous for what she did when she gave lodging to the spies and sent them off in a different direction? (2:25)

There couldn't be two people who serve as polar opposites more than Rahab and Abraham. Revered by Jews, Abraham is known as Father Abraham (John 8:38), the first patriarch, the founder of Judaism, the friend of God, and the prototype man of faith. His spiritual resume is impressive! Rahab, on the other hand, is a Gentile, an immoral woman who lacks scruples, and lives in the wicked city of Jericho. Like Abraham, she had a vibrant faith in God that translated into acts of obedience. She hid the spies in her home (Jos 2:4), sent the soldiers that were in pursuit of them in another direction, and lowered them by rope from the roof (Jo 2:15). Her actions were an expression of her living faith. In Jewish tradition she is regarded as a proselyte, and serves as a model of hospitality. In spite of her sleazy reputation, she was declared righteous by God, proving she was in a right standing with the Lord through faith. According to Matthew 1:5 she is in the messianic line of Jesus, and Hebrews 11:31 gives her the honor of being listed as one of the heroes of the faith. Not bad for a prostitute who reformed her ways and placed her faith in God!

The Conclusion of Dead Faith, (2:26)

As the body without the spirit is dead, so faith without deeds is dead. (2:26)

The final conclusion James makes about the kind of faith that saves, directs our attention to Genesis 2:7 where it says: "Then the LORD God formed a man from the dust of the ground and breathed into his nostrils the breath of life, and the man became a living being." A body is nothing but an inanimate object until the "breath of life" energizes the person bringing him to life. In the same way, faith is like an inanimate object—a corpse—if it produces no good deeds. Acts of obedience are like the breath of life that animates one's faith. The conclusion is inescapable: faith without works is like a rotting corpse. On the other hand, faith that produces works is alive and well!

Insights and Application, (2:14-26)

In my experience, I've discovered that Christians often get hung up on the relationship between faith and works. Salvation is exclusively by faith in Christ alone, and has nothing to do with works. One can't earn salvation by being a good person, or doing good deeds. However, the person who is truly born again is one who has experienced a transformation of his life, the proof of which is seen in the good deeds he commits. If one is truly saved by grace through faith, he will be doing good works. James says that faith without works is dead (2:17) and isn't real saving faith.

The apostle Paul made it clear in Ephesians 2:8-10, that the result of true saving faith is a life that is characterized by good works:

> For it is by grace you have been saved, through faith—and this is not from yourselves, it is the gift of God—[9]not by works, so that no one can boast. [10]For we are God's handiwork, created in Christ Jesus to do good works, which God prepared in advance for us to do.

In the above passage, Paul makes it clear that the sinner is saved by grace through faith for the purpose of doing good works, which is essentially the same thing that James is saying.

In no way is James or Paul advocating a works gospel—as if God accepts the sinner on the basis of good deeds! Like Paul, he's saying that the one who is born again will demonstrate that reality through the good works that flow out of his walk with the Lord. The apostle John offered his readers a way of validating their faith and giving them assurance of their salvation in 1 John 2:3-6:

> We know that we have come to know him if we keep his commands. [4]Whoever says, "I know him," but does not do what he commands is a liar, and the truth is not in that person. [5]But if anyone obeys his word, love for God is truly made complete in them. This is how we know we are in him: [6]Whoever claims to live in him must live as Jesus did.

How does a person know that they know God? They keep his commands by doing good works. They have the desire to emulate the life of Jesus. John is saying the same thing that Paul and James are saying about the relationship between faith and works; namely when someone truly knows God (is born again) they will live an obedient lifestyle, which is another way of saying they are committed to doing good works. On the other hand, if someone claims to know God, but there is no evidence of living an obedient life, John says that person is a liar and the truth is not in him. James says that kind of faith is dead—it doesn't save! Paul might say this individual's faith is sterile because he doesn't have the Spirit, who leads the believer to do good works (Ro 8:12-13).

There are many people who live in doubt about their status with God. In fact, having been in ministry for 30 years, it isn't uncommon for someone in my congregation to sit down with me and tell me that they aren't sure if they are really saved. They lack assurance of their salvation and are unsettled in their spirit because of that. Whenever someone comes to me asking for counsel regarding how they can be sure that they are a true believer, I always direct them back to the time when they asked Jesus into their heart and experienced the new birth. I challenge them to think about what changes became evident in their life after they believed in Jesus. Was there a desire to read the Bible, go to church, listen to Christian music, pray, hang out with other believers, treat people differently, etc. If they can't identify any noticeable change after inviting Jesus into their heart, I have to conclude they probably aren't born again. Their faith wasn't saving faith it was dead faith.

Many years ago I spent a day at Folsom Lake talking with a friend of mine who attended the church I pastored. He told me about someone he knew at work who claims to be a Christian, possessing good knowledge of the Bible, and clearly understands the gospel, but has no desire to live the life of a disciple of Christ. He believes that when he dies he's going to heaven, but in the mean time he has no desire to live the life that Scripture advocates. He doesn't attend church, and quite frankly wants nothing to do with God's people, nor does he feel there is anything wrong with drinking, smoking and partying. This guy has a problem! The faith he claims to have is not the type of faith that James says would save him—it is dead! John would say the truth isn't in him, he's a liar (1 John 2:4). Paul would probably say that he hasn't been regenerated by the Spirit (Titus 3:5).

The true disciple of Christ will display evidence of the new birth by doing good works that flow out of the love he has for the Lord, the degree of which varies from person-to-person. Every believer needs to have assurance of their salvation, or be confident in knowing that they are born again. The best evidence is to consider the change that occurred in your life when you invited the Lord Jesus into your heart.

James and Paul On Justification by Faith: Context is Everything!

There is an apparent tension between what James and Paul say regarding justification by faith. Understanding the context from which each author writes brings clarity to the issue at hand, and helps us not to see the two theologians at odds with each other.

The apostle Paul was often times doing battle against false teachers who were advocating that salvation was by faith in Jesus along with keeping the law (Gal 2:16). Paul would have none of that! He made it clear that justification—the sinner's acquittal—is by faith alone, having nothing to do with keeping the law. Paul speaks of justification by faith from the perspective of initial entrance into the body of Christ—the beginning of one's life as a disciple of Christ.

James, on the other hand, writes from an entirely different perspective. He is describing the results of the sinner being justified by faith. The proof of one's faith, after initial justification, is radical acts of obedience! The type of obedience that was typical of Abraham and Rahab! When James says that a person is justified by works and not by faith alone (2:24), he is isn't contradicting Paul. James is saying that when a person commits radical acts of obedience, it validates their initial entrance into the body of Christ, when they were justified by faith alone. Radical acts of obedience that a disciple of Christ does verify the reality of their initial justification by faith. That is the sense in which he says a person is justified by works and not by faith alone.

In summary, Paul writes about justification by faith from the perspective of initial entrance into the body of Christ, while James writes from the perspective of citing the results of initial justification by faith—radical acts of obedience. Faith and works are inseparably linked together. When you feel God is laying something on your heart, respond in radical obedience like Abraham. Reading about the hero's of the faith (Heb 11) reveals they responded to what the Lord told them to do, and proved the reality of their faith.

This passage should cause the believer to consider being radical for Jesus! True faith can't be held back! Take a chance, and step out in faith and do something great for God!

CHAPTER TEN

"THE POWER OF WORDS"

James 3:1-12

Not many of you should become teachers, my fellow believers, because you know that we who teach will be judged more strictly. ²We all stumble in many ways. Anyone who is never at fault in what they say is perfect, able to keep their whole body in check.

When we put bits into the mouths of horses to make them obey us, we can turn the whole animal. ⁴Or take ships as an example. Although they are so large and are driven by strong winds, they are steered by a very small rudder wherever the pilot wants to go. ⁵Likewise, the tongue is a small part of the body, but it makes great boasts. Consider what a great forest is set on fire by a small spark. ⁶The tongue also is a fire, a world of evil among the parts of the body. It corrupts the whole body, sets the whole course of one's life on fire, and is itself set on fire by hell.

All kinds of animals, birds, reptiles and sea creatures are being tamed and have been tamed by mankind, ⁸but no

human being can tame the tongue. It is a restless evil, full of deadly poison.

With the tongue we praise our Lord and Father, and with it we curse human beings, who have been made in God's likeness. ¹⁰Out of the same mouth come praise and cursing. My brothers and sisters, this should not be. ¹¹Can both fresh water and salt water flow from the same spring? ¹²My brothers and sisters, can a fig tree bear olives, or a grapevine bear figs? Neither can a salt spring produce fresh water.

The obvious topic of discussion in chapter 3:1-12 is the difficulty of controlling one's speech. The potential to stumble and sin with words is greater than all other aspects of our humanity. Great debate exists among commentators as to whether the entire 12 verses are directed to those who desired to be teachers, or if James is using those who were seeking that position as a launching point to address the issue of the uncontrollability of the tongue for all believers. The position of this author is the latter view. James offers a word of caution to those who were seeking to be teachers, then goes into a fuller discourse that has application to all believers.

A Word of Caution to Teachers, (3:1-2)

Not many of you should become teachers, my fellow believers, because you know that we who teach will be judged more strictly. ²We all stumble in many ways. Anyone who is never at fault in what they say is perfect, able to keep their whole body in check. (3:1-2)

Teaching is a spiritual gift that is given to some people in the body of Christ (Ro 12:8, 1 Cor 12:28, Eph 4:11). God has gifted some people to expound his word, making it clear and understandable to the body of Christ. Not everyone has this spiritual gift. James says "not many" of you should presume to be teachers, implying that the gift is probably not widely distributed in the body of Christ. It is likely that some people in the community of faith were seeking to be teachers, but weren't qualified to be in that position because they didn't have the spiritual gift to teach, or didn't have a lifestyle that was conducive to one holding that high a position in the church.

In the first Century there were little, if any, opportunities for advancement and upward mobility. Most people were very poor and ended up staying in the position that they were born into. Since James was writing to Jewish Christians, it is probable that many equated being a teacher with being a rabbi, which was a highly respected position in Jewish culture. People who were of no esteem in the world's eye, but possessed the gift of teaching would become people of great influence in the church, gaining the respect of those they taught. Thus, if God blessed someone with the gift of teaching that was a "nobody" in their culture, they would become a "somebody" in the community of faith.

It appears as though the situation James is addressing involves people who desired to elevate their popularity and social standing among their fellow believers by stepping into a teaching role. However, they didn't have the gift of teaching and probably weren't living a lifestyle that reflected one who holds the position of teacher in the body of Christ. Scripture informs us that before stepping into a teaching role one must study himself approved (2 Tim 2:15) and guard the sacred deposit of the gospel (2 Tim 1:14). In other words, people shouldn't be quick to jump into the role of teacher if they don't know the Scriptures, and aren't living a life worthy of teaching other believers.

The reason people should be cautious about being teachers is that they will be judged more strictly. Teachers are in a position to greatly assist people in their spiritual development through sound biblical exposition, but they are also in a position to do much damage to believers by not handling accurately the word of truth. On judgment day teachers have to give an account of their teaching role (1 Cor 3:12-15). Because of their position of influence over other believers they will be judged more strictly. This truth should give people a moment a pause and reflection before they try to abruptly assume a position of instructing God's people.

Teachers must not only handle the word of God accurately, they must walk in the light they have and be good stewards of the knowledge they possess (1 Cor 4:2). James is not issuing forth a "scare tactic" as much as he is offering a word of caution and pause to those who want to rush into a teaching position for reasons that are suspect. People who want to serve for personal recognition and elevate their status in the church are doing so with wrong motives. At the judgment seat of Christ (2 Cor 5:10) the teacher will not only have to give an account of his teaching, even his motives will come under close scrutiny by the Lord (1 Cor 4:5). His judgment will be more strict because of the position of influence that he occupies. This is another reason to stop and think about it before pursuing a teaching position.

Conversely, the teacher can be in a position to be rewarded greatly on judgment day, if he has discharged his instructing duties faithfully and edified many Christians that sat under his teaching. On judgment day the Lord will find him worthy of being rewarded, because of his diligence in handling the sacred Scriptures and building up God's people.

Verse two provides another reason why would-be teachers should stop and think about it before they seek the position. Teaching is done in the verbal medium, and James introduces the topic of the difficulty people have in controlling their tongue. This puts teachers in harms way because they teach in the verbal medium.

The understatement of fallen humanity is "we all stumble in many ways." Yes, fallen humanity is subject to a multitude of sinful tendencies and infractions. Any believer who is honest with himself will testify to the many ways in which he has stumbled, and be acutely aware of his weaknesses. Of the many ways one can stumble, James focuses specifically on the area of communication: If anyone is never at fault in what he says, he is a perfect man, able to keep his whole body in check (v. 2). If one is never at fault in his communication he would be perfect; having mastery over his entire body. In other words, if we can control what we say, we can control our actions. Controlling our words is thus, the measure that James presents of the perfect man. If the tongue can be mastered, then it's smooth sailing from there. The believer could also keep his passions, emotions, angry outbursts, and other sinful tendencies in check.

Words have their origin in the recesses of the human heart. Jesus said, "For the mouth speaks what the heart is full of." (Mat 12:34b). Words people speak are a reflection of what's in their heart. When Jesus was questioned by the Pharisees about practices that make a person unclean he made it clear that the root of uncleanness is what comes from the human heart, not things from outside a man:

> He went on: "What comes out of a person is what defiles them. 21For it is from within, out of a person's heart, that evil thoughts come—sexual

immorality, theft, murder, [22]adultery, greed, malice, deceit, lewdness, envy, slander, arrogance and folly. [23]All these evils come from inside and defile a person." (Mark 7:20-23)

Given the total depravity of the human heart the potential exists for many verbal sins to be committed. This should cause those seeking to be teachers to have a moment of pause and reflection before they step into that role.

James is now going to expound on the uncontrollability of the tongue, which is directed not just at those desiring to be teachers, but to all believers because the tongue is an area that all Christians need to work on!

The Tongue Navigates Us Through Life, (3:3-6)

When we put bits into the mouths of horses to make them obey us, we can turn the whole animal. [4]Or take ships as an example. Although they are so large and are driven by strong winds, they are steered by a very small rudder wherever the pilot wants to go. [5]Likewise, the tongue is a small part of the body, but it makes great boasts. Consider what a great forest is set on fire by a small spark. [6]The tongue also is a fire, a world of evil among the parts of the body. It corrupts the whole body, sets the whole course of one's life on fire, and is itself set on fire by hell. (3:3-6)

Once again James utilizes colorful illustrations to make his spiritual points. There is an obvious contrast between the size of the horse and the bit in his mouth that steers the animal. The horse is a large powerful animal, yet the small bit causes the horse to go where the rider steers him. A large ship is steered by a small rudder. The influence of the bit and the rudder in controlling the horse and the ship respectively can't be understated. Without the bit in the horse's mouth the rider can't keep the horse on the trail, and the absence of a rudder causes the ship to hopelessly drift in the current and be blown by the wind. They would never reach their destination. Without the bit and the rudder they are without a navigation system and out of control.

The tongue is also a small part of the body (3:5a) but has the ability to steer a person's life. If one has the ability to control his tongue and set forth thoughtful and appropriate communication he can stay out of trouble. Often times, people get into difficult circumstances because of words spoken harshly, thoughtlessly, and impulsively which bring offenses to others. That is the sense in which the tongue makes great boasts. It is one of the smallest body parts, but has great influence over the direction of a person's life.

James utilizes the word picture of a fire for his third illustration: "a great forest fire is started by a small spark" (3:5b). The illustration again plays on the theme of the contrast in size— the small spark results in a big raging fire. Not only that, but once a fire starts raging into a full on forest fire it is virtually uncontrollable! When utilized correctly fire is a useful thing, but when it is out of control it has the potential to wreck havoc! Thousands of acres go up in smoke in a matter of hours. Likewise, when the tongue is utilized correctly communication can enhance relationships, but when words are carelessly spoken they can cause much pain and relationships can go up in smoke.

The tongue is also a fire, a world of evil among the parts of the body (3:6), in the sense that it has potential to accomplish much destruction—like a forest fire. The image of a spreading fire brings to mind gossip that spreads through the church like a forest fire. Consider a slanderous accusation made without foundation against a church leader that spreads like fire damaging his reputation and ministry. The image of a fire is apropos for describing the effects of sinful communication because speech, like fire, has the attribute of destructiveness and spreads rapidly.

The tongue is a world of evil among the parts of the body (3:6). This testifies to the multitude of ways that our speech can be sinful, and points to the destructive power of communication when not used properly. The tongue represents the world of unrighteous thinking and behavior that originates in the depraved human heart.

The book of Proverbs has much to say about the destructive capability of our speech, as well as the pacifying and healing nature of our words. Consider some of the passages from the book of Proverbs that speak to the power of our words:

> **Proverbs 16:27-28:** A scoundrel plots evil, and on their lips it is like a scorching fire. [28]A perverse person stirs up conflict, and a gossip separates close friends.

> **Proverbs 21:23:** Those who guard their mouths and their tongues keep themselves from calamity.

> **Proverbs 16:23:** The hearts of the wise make their mouths prudent, and their lips promote instruction.

> **Proverbs 17:14:** Starting a quarrel is like breaching a dam; so drop the matter before a dispute breaks out.

Proverbs 10:19-21: Sin is not ended by multiplying words, but the prudent hold their tongues. ²⁰The tongue of the righteous is choice silver, but the heart of the wicked is of little value. ²¹The lips of the righteous nourish many, but fools die for lack of sense.

Proverbs 18:19: A brother wronged is more unyielding than a fortified city; disputes are like the barred gates of a citadel.

Proverbs 12:18: The words of the reckless pierce like swords, but the tongue of the wise brings healing.

Proverbs 10:21: The lips of the righteous nourish many, but fools die for lack of sense.

Proverbs 17:27-28: The one who has knowledge uses words with restraint, and whoever has understanding is even-tempered. ²⁸Even fools are thought wise if they keep silent, and discerning if they hold their tongues.

Proverbs 6:16-19: There are six things the Lord hates, seven that are detestable to him: 17haughty eyes, *a lying tongue*, hands that shed innocent blood, 18a heart that devises wicked schemes, feet that are quick to rush into evil, 19a *false witness who pours out lies and a person who stirs up conflict in the community.* (Italics mine)

Proverbs 17:20: One whose heart is corrupt does not prosper; one whose tongue is perverse falls into trouble.

Proverbs 26:28: A lying tongue hates those it hurts, and a flattering mouth works ruin.

Proverbs 4:23-24: Above all else, guard your heart, for everything you do flows from it. 24Keep your mouth free of perversity; keep corrupt talk far from your lips.

Proverbs 15:1-2: A gentle answer turns away wrath, but a harsh word stirs up anger. 2The tongue of the wise adorns knowledge, but the mouth of the fool gushes folly.

Proverbs 15:4: The soothing tongue is a tree of life, but a perverse tongue crushes the spirit.

An examination of these passages reveals both the destructive and constructive potential of our communication with others. It is likely that James has some of these passages from Proverbs in mind as he wrote chapter three.

The tongue corrupts the person and sets the course of his life on fire (3:6). The Greek word *spiloo* is translated "corrupts" in English. The word has religious overtones and carries with it the idea of being defiled, stained, or polluted by sinful activity. Like walking into a room of smokers, second-hand smoke will contaminate you. Your lungs fill up with smoke and the smell gets into your clothing. Thus, you are defiled. In the same way evil words have the capability of defiling the speaker and everyone around them.

One reflection of a person's walk with the Lord is the level of purity in his speech. A Spirit-filled believer who has foul language is a contradiction in terms! The person whose communication is out of control has a spiritual problem—he is corrupted. If his communication continues to be sinful it sets the course of his life on fire, in the sense that damage will result. The person whose mouth is out of control is like a fire-breathing dragon causing destruction wherever he goes.

The tongue is "set on fire by hell". The word translated hell is *gehenna*, which is the Greek form of the Hebrew phrase Valley of Hinnom. It was there that the people of Israel sacrificed their children to the pagan god Molech, by throwing them into the fire bringing God's harsh judgment upon them (Lev 20:2-5, 2 Kings 23:10, Jer 32:35). In Bible days the valley of Hinnom was a garbage dump with fires burning 24 7. If one stood on top of the south wall of Jerusalem he could see the fires burning at night, which became a symbol for hell—the final place of judgment for Satan and his battalions of evil. The point James is making is that sinful communication can be influenced by Satan himself. In other words, sinful communication can be demonic! Satan loves to hear people take the Lord's name in vain, heap verbal abuse on others, and angry shouting matches where people usually regret what they've said after things calm down.

The Untamability of the Tongue, (3:7-8)

All kinds of animals, birds, reptiles and sea creatures are being tamed and have been tamed by mankind, [8]but no human being can tame the tongue. It is a restless evil, full of deadly poison. (3:7-8)

James comes to his conclusion. If you go to the circus you can see that animals have been tamed by man. People wrestle alligators, go inside lion cages, and so forth, but the tongue is untamable. Nobody can completely control their communication. James says it is a "restless evil" in the sense that it is never subdued, content, or taking a break! Sinful communication always raises its ugly head, and does some damage when you least expect it. It is also filled with "deadly poison". Perhaps, James has in mind a venomous snake that is restless and lunges forth, sinking his fangs into his victim. Words can be so painful that it's like being bit by a snake. Our words are like fangs injecting deadly poison into our victim. James' conclusion is that our communication is untamable! Only the perfect man can control his speech (3:2), thus all believers will struggle with their selection of words.

The Inconsistent Use of Our Words, (3:9-12)

With the tongue we praise our Lord and Father, and with it we curse human beings, who have been made in God's likeness. ¹⁰Out of the same mouth come praise and cursing. My brothers and sisters, this should not be. ¹¹Can both fresh water and salt water flow from the same spring? ¹²My brothers and sisters, can a fig tree bear olives, or a grapevine bear figs? Neither can a salt spring produce fresh water. (3:9-12)

In addition to the tongue being untamable, it is inconsistently used by believers. We praise the Lord and then we curse men, who are made in God's likeness. When we curse people and say injurious things, we should be mindful that people are made in the image and likeness of God (Gen 1:26-27). Cursing them assaults the image of God they bear! Cursing a fellow believer that is loved by God, adopted into his family and made in his image is an offense to God Himself! Once again, James uses the term "brothers and sisters", indicating family relationships. People in the body of Christ shouldn't be cursing their fellow brothers and sisters in Christ, after they were praising the Lord in church! This is an inconsistent and sinful use of the tongue.

James also wants us to consider what God's intention was in blessing us with the ability to communicate with one another. There was a divine design in giving us language, just as there was a divine intent with all of God's creation. James mentions fresh water springs, figs, grapevines, and salt water springs. These were basic necessities of life for first Century people. A place was considered habitable if water could be found to sustain life. Water was a precious commodity in that part of the world. A spring can't produce fresh water and salt water at the same time. It isn't in the design of a fresh water spring to produce salt water. God did not design a fig tree to bear olives, and a grapevine to bear figs. It isn't in the divine design for that to happen, because God created plants to bear fruit after their own kind (Gen 1:11-12). James reverses the order of the spring mentioned above and points out that a salt-water spring fed by the Mediterranean can't produce fresh water.

The divine design of communication was to praise the Lord, edify one another, and proclaim the gospel, not curse men, tear people down, and speak inappropriately. When our communication is sinful we are going against the divine intention of language in the first place. This should cause the believer to consider that when his speech isn't what it should be, he is violating the divine design of communication as well as being inconsistent in the use of his words.

Insights and Application, (3:1-12)

In any church in America pastors are usually hard up for people to teach Sunday school for children, adults, teens, and find small group leaders for their Bible studies. In fact, from personal experience and many conversations with my colleagues, most churches are never fully staffed, and pastors can always use more people to serve as teachers.

As pastors are recruiting people to serve, do they point out James 3:1-2 issuing a word of caution to them and scare them out of their spiritual wits? Do we show them this passage of Scripture and dissuade them from stepping up to the plate and serving? When a person wants to serve in a teaching capacity, they need to be faithful in their preparation, walking the walk, and have a heart to serve God's people. How much do they need to know before they can teach? Do they need to attend a Christian College and have a Bible degree, or do they just need to be well read in the Scriptures? Every church needs to have some kind of criterion by which they can determine who can occupy the position of teacher.

In today's spiritual climate there are endless supplies of curriculum that can be used to facilitate the job of teaching a Sunday school class, or leading a small group. One can go online and buy DVD series with workbooks, a leaders guide (with all the answers) and everything to make Bible teaching easy. Resources of this nature didn't exist in the first Century world. In fact, Bibles were not published as they are today, so not many people had copies of the Scriptures in their possession.

In spite of all these resources available to the believer, every church needs to have a policy that explains the criteria to be satisfied before they allow someone to teach. Questions that need to be considered by a governing body include: do they need to be members? Do they need to go through a standard training that all new teachers go through in the church? Do they need to be under the supervision of church leaders to monitor their teaching? Who are teachers accountable to? Do they need to have a background check run on them? Do they need to familiarize themselves with the beliefs of their denomination? Do they need to take a test before they teach?

Every church needs to have a system in place that answers these questions. Scripture warns us not to lay hands on anyone too quickly and empower him to teach or occupy a position of leadership (1 Tim 5:22), because the governing body is responsible for the welfare of the flock. The leaders of a church need to know the people they are entrusting with the authority to teach. They need to see their lifestyle, know if they are teachable, submitted to the church authority, and know their doctrine is acceptable.

In putting together a process to screen and train people before they are put in place, caution needs to be taken so that the requirements are not so strict that it becomes virtually impossible for anybody to occupy a teaching position. On the other hand, churches don't want to make it so easy that anybody can step into a role of influence as a teacher. There needs to be a balance between these two extremes.

Failure to have a procedure in place is asking, even begging for trouble! The Bible is filled with warnings about false teachers, and those who reject authority and promote their own agendas leading God's people astray. It is the job of the leadership to safeguard the flock and protect them against people like this. The worst thing a church can do when they are hard up for teachers, is find a warm body with a pulse and put them in a teaching position without knowing anything about them. When we have a system in place to screen, recruit new leaders and train them with accountability we can be spared much heartache and pain.

I believe James is issuing this warning to people who sought a teaching position for personal prestige and recognition, without being qualified to occupy that position. If their intention is to exercise influence over people so they can be in the limelight and gain personal recognition, then their motives are less than pure.

In v. 2, James indicates that the measure of perfection is the ability to control one's communication. If a believer can keep his speech perfectly controlled, than everything else is a downhill ride. Given the fact that we all have moments of embarrassment when we speak before we think and put our foot in our mouth, this verse should humble us, for it points out an obvious weakness that we all share in common!

In vv. 3-8, James utilizes many word pictures to point out spiritual truths about the tongue. Bits and rudders are necessary to keep horses and ships on course. The tongue is a guiding force in a person's life. Our words can get us in a lot of trouble or they can give us great favor with other people. Consider the following illustration:

I once knew a guy named John. When I met him he was without work and living on unemployment. As I got to know him I discovered that he had a very bad reputation and was known for his outbursts of shouting at people, saying very derogatory things. He informed me that in several previous jobs he was fired because he would "lip-off" to his supervisors and coworkers. At church, he gave his pastors a hard time and had a terrible reputation in some of the fellowships he attended because of his mouth. John serves as the classic example of a guy whose mouth was out of control, constantly getting him in trouble. His inability to control his speech led him down a path of heartache and pain. He couldn't keep a job, stay in a church, or have long-term relationships all because of his mouth! His life went off course because of his inability to speak appropriately to people.

The tongue is compared to a raging forest fire (3:5). Having pastored for many years, I've become aware of how quickly gossip can spread through a church. I believe the most destructive sin in a church is gossip! It spreads quickly and wreaks havoc just like a raging forest fire. I once knew a pastor who resigned his position after years of heartache and pain because of a piece of gossip that spread throughout his church. The pastor had made a number of significant changes when he assumed the pastorate, which included embarking on a building program, initiating new outreach strategies that were bearing fruit and brought new converts into the church. Everything was going along well until a woman in the church made an accusation against him to the board of elders indicating that he had an affair. She was also free with her mouth to spread this accusation throughout the church, and quickly it became the talk of the fellowship, spreading like fire.

In an attempt to squelch the gossip, the elders became fire fighters and tried to extinguish the flames. They questioned the pastor about the accusations and he firmly denied the allegations made against him. A committee was put together to investigate the charges, which took a great deal of time, and many man-hours were logged in by the committee members. The strain that this put on his marriage was severe! Even though the investigation yielded the result that no wrongdoing could be proven on his part, the pastor and his wife suffered greatly and so did the church.

Mistrust and suspicion set in the minds of some people, which led to a number of families leaving to find a new church to attend. Finally, the pastor had enough and felt the best thing for all parties concerned was to resign and move on to another ministry. He swore that this would be the last time that he would ever pastor a church, and went on to take a position as the director of a Christian camp.

Sometime after he resigned he got a phone call from the woman who had made the accusation against him. To his amazement she apologized to him and asked for forgiveness for fabricating the accusations she made. When asked why she made up these vicious lies and put him and his family through so much agony, she explained that she didn't like some of the changes that he was bringing to the church, and didn't want to see the church she attended for many years go in a different direction. She fabricated the lies to get him kicked out, so the church would remain as it had always been.

Having been a long-time member for a good part of her life she couldn't bear to see it change! The pastor forgave her, however the damaging effects on the church and on his family lingered on. The point of this illustration is that the damage that came from one accusation is like a spark that spreads into a fire and brings destruction. The pain that came from this accusation was off the charts! No wonder that James claims that communication can be so evil that there can be a demonic quality to the words we speak.

Going to the circus reveals man's ability to exercise dominion over the earth and tame the animals, but James points out that the tongue is untamable (3:7-8). It is a restless evil filled with deadly poison. Words are venomous and have the ability to inflict lethal bites into people's emotions. The old saying sticks and stones can break my bones but names can never hurt me is dead wrong! Emotional scars take far longer to heal than do physical ones. Some people live in an environment where they constantly hear negative talk. Their parents tell them that they will never amount to anything. Kids pick on them on the playground saying hurtful things like you're ugly, you're stupid, or you're a fat cow, and so forth! These words inflict wounds like deadly poison, and stay with a person for years, marring their self-image, and assaulting their level of self-confidence.

When you listen to kids talk to each other it doesn't take long to discern how brutal their words can be!

Communication is one of the most inconsistent areas of a believer's life (3:9-11). One moment we sit in church praising the Lord, saying Amen(!), in response to the preacher's discourse. Five minutes after the service, we're driving home in our cars trash-talking and gossiping about people in the church while our kids are listening to us verbally assault the people we just worshiped with. How more inconsistent can a believer be in the use of their words than that!

The solution to inconsistent speech is to have Spirit-filled communication! Our speech needs to be under the control of the Holy Spirit. One of the characteristics of the Spirit-filled believer is that his speech will be influenced by the Spirit, as the apostle Paul points our in Ephesians 5:18-19:

> Do not get drunk on wine, which leads to debauchery. Instead, be filled with the Spirit, [19]speaking to one another with psalms, hymns, and songs from the Spirit. Sing and make music from your heart to the Lord, [20]always giving thanks to God the Father for everything, in the name of our Lord Jesus Christ.

The above passage indicates that once filled with the Spirit, the Christian will display evidence of the filling through his communication. Conversely, Ephesians 4:29-30 informs the reader that unwholesome speech has a harmful effect on our relationship with the Spirit:

> Do not let any unwholesome talk come out of your mouths, but only what is helpful for building others up according to their needs, that it may

benefit those who listen. [30]And do not grieve the
Holy Spirit of God, with whom you were sealed
for the day of redemption.

Unwholesome talk includes a wide range of things from
sarcasm, name-calling, filthy language, taking the Lord's name
in vain, dirty jokes, and so forth. The result is clear—the Spirit
can be grieved by improper language.

The intent of language is to bless people, edify those in our
presence, speak truthfully to one another in love, and spread
the gospel. Our words and thoughts are a reflection of what's
in our hearts, and serve as a barometer of our spiritual
condition. Our inability to be what we should be in the area of
our communication should serve as a humbling experience,
because it keeps us aware of our fallen humanity—informing
us of the need to depend on the Lord for help. We all have
a challenge before us to improve in the area of our personal
communication.

Chapter Eleven

"Wisdom From Above and Below"

James 3:13-18

Who is wise and understanding among you? Let them show it by their good life, by deeds done in the humility that comes from wisdom. [14]But if you harbor bitter envy and selfish ambition in your hearts, do not boast about it or deny the truth. [15]Such "wisdom" does not come down from heaven but is earthly, unspiritual, demonic. [16]For where you have envy and selfish ambition, there you find disorder and every evil practice. [17]But the wisdom that comes from heaven is first of all pure; then peace-loving, considerate, submissive, full of mercy and good fruit, impartial and sincere. [18]Peacemakers who sow in peace reap a harvest of righteousness.

Wisdom is a critical concept for James and Jews in general. The wise man is one who has the ability to be intelligent in everyday practical matters. Wisdom wasn't theoretical in nature, it was a quality of spiritual life that translated into practical living. James describes the fruit that is produced by those who walk in the wisdom that comes from above, versus the fruit that comes from walking in the wisdom that comes from below. If there is a connection between the present section and the preceding one, it would be the theme of inconsistency. Believers can display gross inconsistencies in their communication, as well as in the wisdom they function with. The wisdom from below is filled with strife, tension, and envy, which results in fractured relationships. Those who walk in the wisdom from above preserve relationships while bringing peace where none exists. The problem of congregational strife and dissension that came to pass because of sinful communication can be resolved by operating in the right kind of wisdom.

The Wise Man Demonstrates His Wisdom, (3:13)

Who is wise and understanding among you? Let them show it by their good life, by deeds done in the humility that comes from wisdom.

When James asks the question "Who is wise and understanding among you?", that is another way of asking, "Who are the mature believers among you?" Mature believers should be wise in their dealings with people. The word *sophos* (translated wisdom) represents a quality of spiritual life that translated into practical living. In other words, the one who possessed the ability to live out the Scriptures in everyday life in a practical manner was considered to be wise.

The word *epistemon* (translated understanding) is found only here in the New Testament and refers to a highly skilled craftsman, professional tradesman, or an expert in a certain field. Most likely James intends the words to be used synonymously here, but they do carry a slightly different nuance. The wise and understanding person is, therefore, one who is excelling in the Christian life and is bearing fruit as Jesus' disciple.

The demonstration of wisdom and understanding will occur in the way one lives his life. James says "Let him show it by his good life, by deeds done in the humility that comes from wisdom." Wise and understanding people display appropriate behavior, which consists of good deeds done in humility. The word *prautes* (translated humility) often comes into English as "meek", or "gentle". The English terms may connote weakness and be regarded in a negative way, because one can hardly see anything virtuous about being meek or gentle! The Greek term however, carries with it the idea of strength under control.

The term *prautes* was used of horses that were broken so they would be under the control of the rider. There is nothing wimpish about a horse; they are powerful animals. The person who possesses this virtue will have the ability to remain stable, and controlled even in some of the most difficult circumstances that may prevail in his life. Understood this way, James seems to be concerned not so much with faith producing good works in the believer, as much as he is saying that one's good works should show the virtue of meekness (*prautes*) and reflect one's wisdom.

This term gentleness (*prautes*) is also a fruit of the Spirit (Gal 5:23), and was utilized by James in 1:21 where he said: Therefore, get rid of all moral filth and the evil that is so prevalent and humbly (*prautes*) accept the word planted in you, which can save you. Jesus used a form of this word when he said, "Take my yoke upon you and learn from me, for I am gentle (*praos*) and humble in heart, and you will find rest for your souls (Mat 11:29)." That Jesus possesses the virtue of gentleness should be of great comfort to believers, because He doesn't blow up at us every time we make a mistake. He is a controlled presence in our lives, that offers his disciples rest for their souls. To summarize, being meek, gentle, or humble is to be considered a great virtue of the Christian. Doing good works in a meek or gentle spirit is a character trait that indicates wisdom is present.

One who possesses this virtue will not go about his daily business displaying the vices of prideful arrogance, and do things for personal recognition. That behavior would stand in stark contrast to meekness, that the wise person should possess.

The Wisdom That is Not From God, (3:14-15)

But if you harbor bitter envy and selfish ambition in your hearts, do not boast about it or deny the truth. ¹⁵Such "wisdom" does not come down from heaven but is earthly, unspiritual, demonic.

Now James is going to describe the wisdom that does not find its origin in God. Bitter envy and selfish ambition are two vices to be avoided by believers. Envy or jealousy is bad enough, but "bitter envy" is the worst kind of jealousy. When someone has this sin in his heart they are controlled by a need to outdo everybody, and are driven by a need to one-up the competition. Rather than rejoicing over someone's successes they feel threatened, and may covet the accomplishments or talents of another person. This can lead to a poisoning of their spirit with bitter envy.

Along with bitter envy James mentions selfish ambition (*eritheia*), which carries with it the meaning of strife, factionalism, and contentiousness. This word was often used to describe politicians that would promote their own agendas at any expense so they could get elected. If a person is driven by bitter envy and selfish ambition, they are a lethal weapon in the hand of the enemy! One can be sure their behavior will promote division and strife. The problem is in the heart where these vices are harbored. Things seem to always boil-down to the human heart, and its corruption!

The one who possesses these two vices should "not boast about it or deny the truth." The sense in which they are boasting regards their claim to be wise people. They have a puffed up overinflated estimation of themselves and come across arrogantly. The manner in which they deny the truth refers to the fact that they are living a lie. How can one who is filled with bitter envy, selfish ambition, and is boasting about their superior wisdom be telling the truth? Their life testifies to the fact that they are not what they should be before God, and that they are living in denial of their appalling spiritual condition.

James directs our attention to the source of this type of wisdom. It is interesting that he refers to the above mentioned behavior as wisdom at all! From the world's perspective it is considered wise virtuous behavior, but Christians stand diametrically opposed to this type of conduct. That is why James makes it clear that the source of this type of wisdom isn't heaven—it is not the wisdom that would be found in a man who is filled with the Spirit. Its source is from below and is characterized as earthly, unspiritual, and demonic.

Wisdom that is of the earth is a man-centered approach to life that filters God out of the equation. In so doing, man misses the real wisdom that comes only from God, and lives out a pseudo-wisdom—a lie. This is the essence of secular humanism, which is a world view that writes God out of the picture, and places all the glory entirely on man.

Wisdom from below is natural *(psuchikos)* and refers to man in his fallen state—governed by his sensual passions. Man in this condition lacks the ability to comprehend the things of the Spirit of God. Paul said in 1 Corinthians 2:14:

> The person without the Spirit *(psuchikos-the natural man)* does not accept the things that come from the Spirit of God but considers them foolishness, and cannot understand them, because they are discerned only through the Spirit.

This individual doesn't grasp the virtuous nature of meekness and good deeds, he rather advocates selfish ambition, bitter envy, pride, and lives blinded to God's truth.

Wisdom from below is demonic! James seems to be getting worse as he goes. Although James mentions the wisdom from below is earthly and unspiritual, the real villain is Satan— the archenemy of God. He has been behind every distortion of God's revealed truth through the millennia. Satan stands diametrically opposed to the truth of God's Word, his ways, and offers his own brand of spiritually. If we go back to 3:6 where James linked the tongue to hell *(gehenna)*, we see how he has prepared us for linking wisdom from below with the demonic realm.

Putting together the world, flesh, and the Devil James seems to have identified the unholy Trinity—a wicked combination that can result in numerous evil practices. Now that James has identified the source and characteristics of the wisdom from below, he is going to describe its fruit.

The Fruit of Wisdom From Below, (3:16)

For where you have envy and selfish ambition, there you find disorder and every evil practice.

Where envy and selfish ambition is the driving force behind people's behavior, you can be assured that the world, flesh, and the Devil are large and in charge! The fruit of the wisdom from below is "disorder and every evil practice". When God's wisdom is absent there will be chaos, division, splits, church fights, and so forth, in the community of faith. The word *akatastasia* (translated disorder) carries with it the idea of instability, a state of confusion, a disturbance, or a tumult. James used this word to describe the double-minded man *unstable* in all his ways (1:8), and described the tongue as a *restless* evil and full of deadly poison (3:8). Paul mentioned that God is not a God of *disorder*, but of peace (1 Cor 14:33).

Disorder was running rampant in the community of faith, and was being accompanied by every "evil practice", which is the translation of the Greek word *phaulos*. This word is used to contrast the saved from the unsaved (John 5:29, Rom 9:11, 2 Cor 5:10) and it refers to evil that is worthless, vile, and contemptible. Since James mentions "every evil practice" he is referring not to specific sins, but to a wide range of worthless behavior that has its origin in human wisdom and wrecks havoc wherever it is found.

This situation in James' congregation is serious and can't be minimized. The seeds of destruction are in the ground, and they are beginning to sprout. If the situation goes unchecked, the community will disintegrate and implode with internal strife. There is a way to correct the situation. Those people who are operating in this type of wisdom must consider the wisdom from above, and align themselves properly with God.

The Wisdom From Above, (3:17-18)

But the wisdom that comes from heaven is first of all pure; then peace-loving, considerate, submissive, full of mercy and good fruit, impartial and sincere. [18]Peacemakers who sow in peace reap a harvest of righteousness.

James is now going to describe the wisdom that comes from heaven—God's wisdom, which, has already been promised to be given generously to all without finding fault when they ask (1:5). He mentions seven characteristics of God's wisdom that every believer should cherish, and every church should display in their fellowship. Is James equating wisdom from heaven with Spirit-produced virtues like the apostle Paul does (Gal 5:22-23)?

Scripture does provide examples of a link between wisdom and the Spirit. For example, Pharaoh noted Joseph's wisdom and the presence of God's Spirit in him (Gen 41:38-39). Bazalel, was filled with the Spirit and given wisdom by God, to empower him to make items for the tabernacle (Ex 31:3). Joshua was filled with the "spirit of wisdom" after Moses laid hands on him (Deu 34:9). In Isaiah's prophecy regarding Jesus he says: "The Spirit of the LORD will rest on him—the Spirit of wisdom and of understanding…(Isa 11:2)."

James is developing his pneumatology utilizing Sophia-based terminology, whereas Paul is writing from a Pentecost-based theology of the Spirit. Both authors are essentially saying the same thing, but using different vocabulary. Certainly, James would acknowledge that the wisdom from above is linked to the Holy Spirit, and Paul would agree that the Spirit-filled believer will display traits of wisdom! In other words, James wisdom-based theology is essentially the same as Paul's Spirit-based theology, the two authors are just using different terminology.

The first wisdom virtue is to be "pure" (*hagnos*). Since it is mentioned first on the list it must carry vital importance. The word connotes something that is undefiled or free from moral contamination. In speaking of the Corinthians Paul said "I promised you to one husband, to Christ, so that I might present you as a pure (*hagnos*) virgin to him (2 Cor 11:2)." This virtue stands in stark contrast to the disorder and every evil practice that typifies the wisdom from below (3:16), and is ripping apart the fellowship. The remedy for the people who are causing the dissension is to repent and stand before God with a pure heart.

The second wisdom virtue is to be "peace-loving" (lit. peaceable). Where the wisdom of God is present, peace will exist in the community rather than strife, and selfish ambition. Paul admonished the Romans in 12:18: "If it is possible, as far as it depends on you, live at peace with everyone." Being at peace with your neighbor, your fellow brothers in Christ, and people in the world is a mark of wisdom. Proverbs 16:7 informs us that godly living does indeed promote peaceful relationships even with one's enemies: "When the LORD takes pleasure in anyone's way, he causes their enemies to make peace with them."

The third wisdom virtue is to be "considerate" (*epieikes*). The difficulty in translating this word is that there is no English equivalent for the Greek term. It carries with it the ideas of goodness, gentleness, courtesy, mildness, benevolence, generosity, forbearing and yielding. It is a virtue that elders should possess (1 Tim 3:3, Titus 3:2), and because of the nearness of the Lord's coming, all believers should display "gentleness" to everyone (Phil 4:5).

Therefore, we conclude this term connotes a gracious acceptance of others who may differ with you. It is a mark of God's wisdom that in the midst of arguments or differences that exist between people, deference is given to others. This is the opposite of the selfish ambition that promotes one's own agenda at the expense of the community of faith. The one who possesses this virtue is not to be viewed as a weak, spineless person who can't assert himself. He is one who preserves peace and unity by being humble, while considering others more important than himself (Phil 2:3).

The fourth wisdom virtue is to be "submissive" (*eupeithes*). The person who displays this quality is compliant and yielding. He is willing to take instruction and correction when necessary. Rather than being overly defensive and inflexible on nonessential matters of theology and practice, he has the ability to promote the greater good of Christians living in unity with each other. Thus, he can yield to the preferences of others and show respect to those who see things differently than he does, such as with food preferences (Ro 14:15).

My friend Gene Smillie made the observation that James manifested these traits in dealing with the issues that came up at the Council of Jerusalem in Acts 15. James himself seemed to be a legalist and devoutly loyal to the Torah-based ceremonies associated with Temple worship, yet he acquiesced gladly to the consensus that emerged in that discussion about Gentile converts' responsibilities in the new community forming around Jesus' apostles. Imagine how disruptive and damaging James could have been to the church had he "dug in" and been unyielding regarding the Gentiles role in the new community of believers.

The fifth wisdom virtue is to show "mercy". One who receives God's mercy is also one who gives mercy to others. Where God's wisdom is present mercy should be found in abundance, for James says "full of mercy." James has already said that judgment without mercy will be shown to anyone who has not been merciful (2:13). Once saved, the believer shows the evidence of a transformed life by being merciful and forgiving to others.

In one of Jesus' parables there was a servant that owed a debt to his master that he couldn't possibly repay. After begging his master he had mercy on him and forgave the debt. However, this servant wouldn't forgive the debt that someone else owed him. The master severely judged the servant for his double standard by saying: "You wicked servant,' he said, 'I canceled all that debt of yours because you begged me to. [33]Shouldn't you have had mercy on your fellow servant just as I had on you (Matt 18:32-33)?" If one receives God's mercy, but is unwilling to give mercy to others, his spiritual life is not what it should be.

The strife and conflict existing in James congregation testified to the lack of mercy, compassion, and love in the hearts of the people. This will be the case when people are filled with bitter envy and selfish ambition, and operate under the wisdom from below.

The sixth wisdom virtue to be displayed is "good fruits". This refers to the good works that a disciple of Christ is to display and should be the product of a living and vibrant faith. James has already discussed the relationship between faith and works (2:14-20), and one can see why James placed mercy and good fruits next to each other. Where mercy exists in the human heart good works will be produced, like that of the Good Samaritan (Luke 10:30-37). Where mercy is lacking, people will appear to be insensitive and indifferent to human suffering.

The seventh wisdom virtue is being "impartial" (*adiakritos*). This is the only occurrence of the word in the New Testament. The word is more literally *not to be divided*; meaning indecisive, inconsistent, or doubtful. Accepting people with a single-minded focus as brothers in Christ without showing favoritism is what James has in mind. He has already wrote against the sin of impartiality (2:1-9), and been clear that where this dreadful sin exists, a violation of the law of love occurs.

The eighth wisdom virtue is to be "sincere" (*anupokritos*), which is more literally translated *without hypocrisy.* Even a superficial reading of the gospels will reveal that Jesus had a serious problem with hypocrisy! He spoke against this sin four times in the Sermon on the Mount (Matt 6:2, 5, 16, 7:5) and harshly condemned the Pharisees for their hypocrisy in Matthew 23. He told them "on the outside you appear to people as righteous but on the inside you are full of hypocrisy and wickedness (Mat 23:28)." They had the appearance of righteousness but in reality it was all an allusion. Where hypocrisy is absent there will be sincerity in one's spiritual experience—no playacting.

The final wisdom virtue on James' list is the "peacemaker", however, James isn't identifying a virtue, he's identifying a person who possesses all the above virtues and thus, is filled with God's wisdom. When all these virtues are found in one person, he will be a peacemaker. In other words, the embodiment of these virtues is the peacemaker. The fruit of God's wisdom is to make and promote peace, rather than division and strife. James uses an agricultural metaphor when he describes peacemakers as people who sow the seed of peace, which yields a harvest of righteousness. Believers who seek to live at peace with everyone by displaying the above virtues, provide fertile ground for the crop of righteousness to develop.

How can people become mature in Christ and live righteously when there is constant strife, division, and discord in their church? James has already informed his readers that the fruit of the wisdom from below is "disorder and every evil practice

(3:16)." When Christians exist in the soil of love and unity with one another, great potential exists for righteous behavior to flourish. Conversely, it is difficult to mature in Christ where there is constant strife, envy, and selfish ambition.

James has identified the problem utilizing wisdom terminology. The offending parties' behavior is driven by the wisdom from below. The solution to this is to repent and function under God's wisdom that comes from above. That is the solution he offers to his readers regarding how to heal the fractured body, but there is more to come in chapter four.

James has contrasted the fruit of the wisdom from below, with the fruit that comes from the wisdom from heaven. When placed side-by-side this is what we have:

Wisdom From Below	**Wisdom From Above**
Bitter Envy	Purity
Selfish ambition	Peace-loving
Boasting	Considerate
Denying the truth	Submissive
Earthly	Merciful
Unspiritual	Good fruit
Demonic	Impartial
Disorder	Sincere
Evil Practices	Righteousness

Insights and Application, (3:13-18)

James asked the question, "Who is wise and understanding among you (v. 16)?" Every believer should ask that question about the people they worship with. It is important for everyone to identify the mature, godly people they congregate with and learn from their example. In today's world it is in vogue for people to have a mentor. Christians can profit by having a mentor who has walked with the Lord for many years, and acquired a great deal of wisdom through a variety of life experiences. All God's people should have a mature Christian that they "hang out" with, to learn from their godly example and provide them with guidance and counsel when it is needed. Having a mentor who is a wise and understanding brother in the Lord is something that every believer can profit from!

For James, wisdom is a quality of spiritual life in Christ. The wise person is the one who doesn't just know the Scriptures, but has the remarkable ability to live them out and make them real in his everyday life. Wisdom is therefore practical, not theoretical. Although James doesn't mention the Holy Spirit in this section, in his thought-life he would consider the one filled with God's wisdom to be a Spirit-filled believer. He is using different vocabulary than Paul to describe basically the same thing—Christians must display behavior that is Christlike! Whether it is described as the fruit of the Spirit, as the apostle Paul does, or being filled with God's wisdom as James does, it means the same thing. The believer's life must be submitted and controlled by God. Whenever God's people grieve the Spirit, rather than walk in the Spirit, they function in worldly wisdom rather than God's wisdom. The result will always be varying degrees of chaos and strife.

It would be easy to say that the one's causing the problems are unbelievers, because they are driven by the wisdom that comes from below. However, James doesn't imply that this is a cut-and-dry case of believers verses nonbelievers! It seems to me that he is referring to Christians! Disciples of Christ aren't always what they should be in their daily experience. When this happens all kinds of conflict can abound, as it did in the church at Corinth. Christians can be out of step with the Spirit, and seem to be functioning under the wisdom from below rather than from above.

It is not uncommon for churches to be rift with conflict! Most pastors at some point in their career will be in a church that goes through some kind of crisis situation. Many believers may attend a church at some point in their life that goes through an awful situation because of unresolved conflict. To say that the ones causing the trouble are nonbelievers isn't fair. Having been in many conflict situations over the years, I have seen some common denominators that appear in turbulent circumstances.

One is the bitter envy James identified, which can be poison in a person's heart. We may be envious of a person's talents, spiritual gifts, status in the church, their marriage, and so forth. This is a sinful attitude that if left unfettered can cause much damage in the person harboring the envy, and in the church. Jealously can lead to giving a cold shoulder, wishing people ill will, and cause people to say and do things that undermine others in the church. The solution to this sinful attitude is to rejoice and thank the Lord for the gifts, and blessings that he has given other people in your church. That is how you cleanse your heart from envy.

Another common denominator in conflict situations is the vice of selfish ambition. This trait exists where people want to get things their way and have control! If they don't get their way, and have a degree of control, they are prone to put up a fight. Most conflict scenarios have at their root bitter envy and selfish ambition.

The third part of the common denominator in conflict situations is the heart! When people's hearts aren't right with God, things can get out of control. I remember my district superintendent visited a small church in conflict on a Sunday morning, for a congregational meeting after the service. Several issues were discussed and the behavior of the people was hostile, with little or no grace displayed—it was brutal! Issues were discussed with little if any resolution. Afterward, the district superintendent, who has been through many of these awful situations, said the problem here is that there is no love. The problem was their hearts! These people displayed no fruit of the Spirit, their sanctification was entirely questionable, and they needed to have a fresh dose of God's love injected in their hearts! I believe that all of the malcontents were believers in Christ, but they sure didn't act like it!

One with even a cursory understanding of Scripture could see the behavior—the backbiting, venomous accusations, insinuations, and hostility weren't coming from God. This was an example of believers who were so grieving the Spirit, that one could conclude their conduct was earthly, unspiritual, and demonic! The fact is, Christians can appear that way at times! Believers need to make sure that their attitudes are right before God, and they are filled with the Spirit. Obviously, that wasn't happening in James' congregation, and it often happens where congregations are rift with conflict in our contemporary situation.

Where people are walking in God's wisdom (Spirit-filled) the result will be peace and harmony. By comparing James' list of wisdom virtues, with Paul's list of Spirit virtues (fruit of the Spirit) we can arrive at the conclusion that both lists contain traits that promote unity, enhance relationships, and provide an environment where people can maximize their growth in Christ. The virtues mentioned in these two lists will be found in people that are in tune with God. Where people possess these virtues, unity and peace will result in the congregation.

James' Wisdom Virtues	**Paul's Fruit of the Spirit**
Pure	Love
Peace-loving	Joy
Considerate	Peace
Submissive	Patience
Mercy	Kindness
Good Fruit	Goodness
Impartial	Faithfulness
Sincere	Gentleness
Peacemakers	Self-control

The ones who embody these traits will be peacemakers. These are not believers who have specialized training in conflict resolution (although some may), they are people who by their actions promote love, acceptance, and forgiveness, thereby creating an environment of unity and harmony in the body of Christ. These are the people who are wise and understanding, showing their wisdom by their good life through deeds done in the humility that comes from wisdom (v. 13). The fruit of their good deeds brings wholeness and unity to the church. Mature believers always work to preserve oneness in the body of Christ.

James has identified peace as a key ingredient of God's wisdom. The nature of this peace is health and wholeness in the church. The peace James has in mind isn't a fake peace, where issues are swept under the carpet and never dealt with, such that a façade of harmony exists with no substance. A healthy body is one that deals with sin, practices church discipline, confronts heresy, and has loving accountability.

When contrasting James' vices that are characteristic of the wisdom from below, with Paul's works of the flesh, some similarities can be noted. Selfish ambition and envy are found in both lists. The works of the flesh that Paul mentions should be typical of unsaved people: however, I again assert that Christians aren't always what they should be! Both lists, when applied to the believer, indicate a massive grieving of the Spirit! It should be obvious that where these vices are displayed in a group of people there will be mass chaos! James identified the fruit of wisdom from below as disorder and every evil practice.

James - Wisdom from Below	Paul – Works of the Flesh
Bitter Envy	Sexual immorality
Selfish ambition	Impurity
Boasting	Debauchery
Denying the truth	Idolatry
Earthly	Witchcraft
Unspiritual	Hatred
Demonic	Discord
Disorder	Jealousy
Evil Practices	Fits of rage
	Selfish ambition
	Dissensions
	Factions
	Envy
	Drunkenness
	Orgies

It should be obvious that the fruit of both lists is chaos, disorder, and broken relationships. The solution for believers who are carrying on this way is to repent of their sinful behavior and walk in the Spirit.

CHAPTER TWELVE

"THE ORIGIN OF CONFLICT"

James 4:1-6

What causes fights and quarrels among you? Don't they come from your desires that battle within you? ²You desire but do not have, so you kill. You covet but you cannot get what you want, so you quarrel and fight. You do not have because you do not ask God. ³When you ask, you do not receive, because you ask with wrong motives, that you may spend what you get on your pleasures. ⁴You adulterous people, don't you know that friendship with the world means enmity against God? Therefore, anyone who chooses to be a friend of the world becomes an enemy of God. ⁵Or do you think Scripture says without reason that he jealously longs for the spirit he has caused to dwell in us? ⁶But he gives us more grace. That is why Scripture says: "God opposes the proud but shows favor to the humble."

Chapter four continues the theme of conflict existing in the church. James has described the difficulty in controlling the tongue and described its destructive capabilities. He has also described the terrible fruit of the wisdom that comes from below. One can see how endless conflict scenarios can rise to the surface because of those things. Now James will add one more aspect to the tinderbox of conflict that existed in his churches. He describes how at the root of every conflict, there are wrong desires that drive human behavior causing all kinds of problems. The language James uses indicates that the problems were serious enough to cause the church to implode, unless the guilty parties repent. This is a classic example of Christians behaving badly! They need to walk away from the worldly wisdom they are accustomed too, and embrace God's wisdom as they repent of their sinful behavior. James will offer instruction on how to do that.

Conflict Originating From Corrupt Desires, (4:1-2b)

What causes fights and quarrels among you? Don't they come from your desires that battle within you? ²You desire but do not have, so you kill. You covet but you cannot get what you want, so you quarrel and fight.

In a church situation where conflict abounds, it would seem natural for the people to wonder what's causing the mess we're in! This is what James does by asking the question, "What causes fights and quarrels among you?" The language James uses is graphic and points to the volatility of the situation. The word *polemos* (translated fights) refers to prolonged disputing or armed combat, and is sometimes translated war (Mat 24:6, Heb 11:34, Rev 11:7, 16:14). The word *mache* (translated quarrels) refers to personal conflicts without weapons, such as angry disputes that turn into shouting matches. Both of these terms can be used metaphorically, which is most likely the case here. The fights and quarrels existing among the people testifies to the fact that they were not walking in God's wisdom, and reaping the fruit of harmony and peace that results when people are in tune with God.

James provides the answer to the question he has proposed: "Don't they come from your desires that battle within you?" The culprit has been identified! The desires (*hedonon*) that battle within you are causing the fights and quarrels. The Greek term refers to one who seeks to gratify the sinful tendencies of fallen man. It is always used in a negative sense in the New Testament. The Greek word *hedonon* is where we get our English word hedonist. A modern-day hedonist is one who lives a lifestyle of seeking pleasure by gratifying every passion and lust imaginable. The apostle Paul refers to sinful desires battling within the believer as the sinful nature (Gal 5:16). He is saying essentially the same thing as James, just using different vocabulary.

People in James congregation were selfishly concerned with gratifying their own sinful desires at the expense of the welfare of the body. The desires are described as "battling within you." James is describing the internal battle that every believer faces. The desires are described as a "battle" within, which translates the Greek word *strateuomenon*, which indicates a raging battle. It is written as a participle, which means the battle is ongoing, suggesting the inner conflict of the believer never comes to an end.

The apostle Paul described this internal battle to do good versus evil in Romans 7:7-25, and Peter describes the inner battle of the believer when he said: Dear friends, I urge you, as aliens and strangers in the world, to abstain from sinful desires, which war against your soul (I Pet 2:11). When we give into our sinful desires we lose the inner battle and pursue behavior that causes conflict in the church. The desire for control, prestige, recognition, power, and so on, begin to be expressed at the expense of the welfare of the church family.

To further explain the meaning of evil desires battling within each individual, James says "You want something *(epithumeo)* but don't get it (v. 2a)." The word *epithumeo*, is usually translated lust, so a more literal translation would be "You lust but don't get what you lust after." Lust can have a positive or negative meaning depending on the context. For example, Paul tells Timothy "if anyone sets his heart on being an overseer, he desires *(epithumeo)* a noble task (1 Tim 3:1)", which would be a positive usage of the word. In the passage under consideration, the lusting is a sinful desire that is not being met, which is causing a knee jerk reaction in the people: You kill and covet, but you cannot have what you want. You quarrel and fight (v. 2b).

Does James intend for his readers to take "kill" literally? Did things deteriorate to the point where people in James congregation were murdering each other? It seems unlikely that James would intend for his audience to take this literally, because if this were happening wouldn't he spend more time talking about this hellacious sin! If this is intended to be taken literally, James would be glossing over and minimizing a horrendous sin. It is better to understand James speaking figuratively, as Jesus did (Mat 5:21-22). However, one can understand how when strong desires are not satisfied, and one person covets what is not rightfully his, violent behavior can result. Perhaps, James is making the point that if you continue down this course, at some point you're going to start killing each other, whether it's with harsh language, shouting matches, or exchanging blows!

James placed killing alongside coveting *(zelos)*. The word *zelos* is often translated zeal or envy. The word can have positive connotations, as when a person has zeal for God, or negative connotations as is found here. The NIV rightly translates the word covet; desiring something that isn't yours and is off-limits. This brings to mind the tenth commandment found in Exodus 20:17:

> You shall not covet your neighbor's house. You shall not covet your neighbor's wife, or his male or female servant, his ox or donkey, or anything that belongs to your neighbor.

In spite of fights and quarrels, mixed with killing and coveting, the people's sinful desires are still unmet, so it leads to more quarreling and fighting. It seems as though the people are spinning their wheels and going nowhere! Even when they turn to prayer that is of little use because it is being done in a sinful manner.

Conflict Originating From Corrupted Prayer, (4:2c-3)

You do not have because you do not ask God. ³When you ask, you do not receive, because you ask with wrong motives, that you may spend what you get on your pleasures.

The unmet desires of the people are attributed to lack of prayer. James doesn't specify what they wanted to have, but we assume from the context that whatever they wanted it wasn't good and pleasing to God. When they do pray their motives are entirely suspect! The reason for seeking God in prayer is to gratify their pleasures (*hedonon*). So corrupt was the prayer life of the guilty parties that they were utilizing prayer as if it were a means of gratifying their hedonistic tendencies. Earlier James mentioned that if anyone lacks wisdom that he could ask God and He would give it to him generously without finding fault (1:5). If they were praying correctly, with proper motivation, there is no reason why God wouldn't make good on his promise to bless them with wisdom, or whatever else they were asking for that lined up with God's purposes.

As it was, the culprits were not seeing much fruit in prayer because they didn't pray often, nor did they pray with right motives. Investing time in conversation with God that focuses on one's pleasures, desires, ambitions, and self-centered pursuits goes against the grain of praying in Jesus' name, for Kingdom advancement.

Conflict Originating From Corrupt Relations With The World, (4:4-6)

You adulterous people, don't you know that friendship with the world means enmity against God? Therefore, anyone who chooses to be a friend of the world becomes an enemy of God. (4:4)

Another aspect of the spiritual problems that existed in James' congregations was their relationship with the world. In language reminiscent of the prophets of old, James addresses their adulterous relationship with the world. When the people of Israel worshiped other gods it was considered to be the act of an unfaithful wife who committed adultery against her God. Isaiah (54:1-6), Jeremiah (2:2, 3:20), Ezekiel (16:15-19), and Hosea (2:2-5, 3:1-5, 9:1) all addressed God's people through the imagery of spiritual adultery. James calls his people "adulterous" because they were having an affair with the world. The church is the bride of Christ, and when God's people get wrapped up in the things of the world this is betrayal of Christ on a grand scale.

The relationship between God and his people has been portrayed through the metaphor of the marriage union. In the Old Testament, when God's people went after other gods, proving their unfaithfulness to the Lord, they violated the covenant. Doing so placed them in a position to receive God's judgment, which had dire consequences. The Israelites suffered much agony that could have been avoided if they had been faithful to God. James' congregations appear to be positioning themselves to receive God's judgment, unless they repent of their worldliness and get in tune with God.

The world represents organized society that writes God out of the picture, and is hostile toward God and his people. If a believer becomes friendly with the world by adopting its values, philosophies, and wisdom, James considers this an expression of hatred toward God! This may seem harsh, but this is James' way of shocking his readers into reality, so they will grasp how serious their sinful behavior has become. It has already been demonstrated that the guilty parties are walking in the wisdom from below, which is energized by the world system (3:13-18).

To provide more shock effect for his readers, James tells them if "anyone chooses to be a friend of the world they become an enemy of God". Like pouring cold water on their faces, James is trying to wake them up and bring them back into spiritual reality by getting them to see the magnitude of their sins. They aren't acting like worshipers of God, they are acting like his enemies. This is serious stuff: spiritual adultery, hatred toward God, and becoming an enemy of God. If this doesn't get their attention, what will? If they continue down this path, God's judgment will be imminent just as it was for the Israelites.

Or do you think Scripture says without reason that he jealously longs for the spirit he has caused to dwell in us? [6]But he gives us more grace. That is why Scripture says: "God opposes the proud but shows favor to the humble." (4:5-6)

Verse five provides the interpreters of Scripture with a challenge. What Scripture is James referring to when he says "the Scripture says without reason?" Secondly, is the "spirit" a reference to the spirit of man, or should the spirit have a capital S indicating a reference to the Holy Spirit? The original manuscripts were written in capital letters so the translators had to determine if the s should be a small "s" or a capital "S". The third difficulty is the manner in which the word "envies" should be understood.

By reviewing several translations of v. 5, different options will unfold to the reader:

> **King James Version:** Do ye think that the scripture saith in vain, the spirit that dwelleth in us lusteth to envy?

The above translation understands "spirit" to be the spirit of man that God breathed in us (Gen 2:7). Because of man's fallen nature, his spirit envies (*phthonos*) in a sinful capacity, which is why people commit spiritual adultery with the world (4:4). This translation points to man's fallen nature as the reason why people are unfaithful to their God. In this understanding *phthonos* (envies) must have a negative connotation because of its association with human sinfulness. The occurrences of *phthonos* in Biblical Greek are never used with reference to God; they all refer to human sinfulness. The reason God gives us grace (v. 6) is to compensate for our human sinfulness by giving us the ability to be faithful to the Lord. Grace overcomes our human frailties and corruptions so that we can be the people God wants us to be.

> **New International Version:** Or do you think Scripture says without reason that he jealously longs for the spirit he has caused to dwell in us?

> **English Standard Version:** Or do you suppose
> it is to no purpose that the Scripture says, "He
> yearns jealously over the spirit that he has made
> to dwell in us"?

The NIV and ESV translations understand God being jealous over the spirit of man that he has made to dwell in us. This is an allusion back to the creation account when God breathed the breath of life into man and he became a living being (Gen 2:7). God is a jealous God in the sense of desiring our full devotion, which he rightly deserves since he is our creator. This understanding of the passage fits perfectly into the flow of the argument. Since James' readers are spiritual adulterers, they must understand that they are offending a jealous God, who desires the obedience of the people He has created. God's jealously (*phthonos*) is to be understood in a positive way. He loves his church and desires our devotion, just as a husband craves the devotion of his bride. That God yearns jealously over his church should be an indicator of how much he loves us, and be a source of comfort to the believer.

> **New Living Translation:** What do you think the
> Scriptures mean when they say that the Holy
> Spirit, whom God has placed within us, jealously
> longs for us to be faithful?

This translation understands "Spirit" to be the Holy Spirit that God placed in us at the moment of our conversion experience. The Holy Spirit is jealous for our faithfulness to Him. If this translation is correct, it is the only direct reference to the Holy Spirit in the entire homily. The grace God gives (4:6) is to empower the believer to be faithful to the Lord. The meaning of the NLT, NIV and ESV are very close because they emphasize divine jealousy, which fits the context of the passage.

Now the question regarding which Scripture is being referred to in v. 5 can be answered. This is the only citation of a Scripture that is unknown. What James appears to be doing is speaking in general terms of a theme that runs throughout the Scripture (God's jealously) rather than citing a specific text. If someone were to say, "Do you think the Scripture says without reason that God loves us?" There would be a mountain of Scripture that could be cited to support the theme of God's love. Therefore, we conclude that James cited the Biblical theme of God's jealously, but offered no specific Biblical text.

Whichever way one understands v. 5, grace is crucial and necessary for God's people to be faithful and overcome their tendency to drift into the world. James cites Proverbs 3:34 from the Septuagint (which is the Greek translation of the Hebrew Bible), as does Peter (1 Pet 5:5). Grace is to be understood in this context, as the God-given power that enables a disciple to satisfy the demands placed upon us by a jealous God. Without it, we would be in a world of weakness—unable to please God!

Christians should covet God's grace and want to keep the channel open to receive an endless supply of the same. The way to do that is by being humble. Humility opens the door to receiving God's grace for godly living. Humility is a key aspect of the wisdom that comes from above that James described in 3:13-18. Humility is one of the essential virtues of the Christian experience! God is always favorably disposed to the humble, for Jesus said, "For all those who exalt themselves will be humbled, and those who humble themselves will be exalted (Luke 14:11)."

The word translated "proud" is *huperephanos*, which is a compound word; *huper* (meaning above) and *phainomai* (meaning to appear or to manifest). Therefore, the meaning of the word is to "appear above others". The proud person is one who loves to place himself above others and occupy a place of preeminence. Recognition, status, and being first above others are of primary importance to the proud man. Having an overestimation of himself, and his abilities causes him to be arrogant and haughty. This is characteristic of the wisdom that comes from below (3:14-16), which should be abhorrent for the man of God.

The one who is filled with pride of this type has a big problem, for "God opposes the proud"! His haughty attitude places him in direct opposition to God. James uses another colorful word picture in this verse. The word "opposes" (*antitassomai*) has military connotations. It depicts an army in a high state of combat readiness— everyone is locked and loaded! James is implying that God has made himself combat-ready against those who walk in prideful ways. This should give us an idea of how offensive the sin of pride is to God.

Pride stands in direct contrast to humility. Rather than trying to place himself above others, the humble man doesn't seek recognition and status. He doesn't have an overinflated estimation of himself, he recognizes his need to depend on God, and acknowledges that all he is, and has, comes from the Lord. The only boasting the humble man does is in what the Lord has done for him. This man embodies the wisdom from above, and has an open channel to God's grace.

Insights and Application, (4:1-6)

This passage has much to offer those who work at resolving conflict scenarios. Who among us never ends up in a touchy situation with someone? Conflict is a normal part of human existence. The root of much conflict that exists in marriages, in the workplace, with friends, and church members is unmet desires (vv. 1-2). People want something to be done their way, but they're not getting what they want, so it drives them to do divisive things! It pushes them over the edge and things get ugly! We can all think of times that we wanted something in a relationship to be done our way, but we didn't get what we wanted, so the relationship ended up poisoned!

The problem with unmet desires is that they must be evaluated to determine whether they are valid desires, or selfishly based desires that don't take into consideration the overall good of the parties concerned! For example, a wife's desire to spend time with her husband is a valid need that the husband must try to meet. If he doesn't their relationship will be strained! Fulfilling valid desires that people have helps to ensure peaceful relationships.

However, when you have two groups of people who carry unmet desires that stand in opposition to each other, look out— trauma is inevitable! Especially when the desires are selfishly motivated, lacking any regard for other people's point of view. Those who are in conflict with someone need to ask themselves what unmet needs within them are triggering the conflict, and evaluate whether or not they are valid or invalid desires. If they are selfishly motivated desires they need to adjust their thinking and let go of their expectations. If, on the other hand, you're the one who is not meeting a valid need in someone you're in a relationship with, it would be wise to make an adjustment and become more sensitive to the needs of the person. This will strengthen the relationship.

Many of the missionaries I've known over the years, have told me that in some of the places they've served prayer meetings were dynamic! God was moving in great ways through new converts, many baptisms were occurring, church attendance was rising, and it appears genuine revival had broken out in their ministry. Prayer meetings were packed—they were bursting at the seams with standing room only! In my experience in leading prayer meetings, they are always the most sparsely attended ministry of the church. It is fair to say that the American church is weak in prayer. When revival breaks out everybody goes to the prayer meeting. Prayer can be a barometer of church health (4:2-3)!

Not only is prayer lacking in the American church, it is often selfishly driven. With the influence of the prosperity gospel, it is not uncommon for believers to be praying selfishly about matters that are far away from the advancement of the gospel. When people are praying more about God improving their lifestyle with more possessions, and more discretionary income, their prayers reflect their hedonistic tendencies. God is like an online shopping mall, where they present their list of wants to him, only to be disappointed later on because they didn't get their prayers answered as they expected. The instructions the Lord gave his disciples was to pray in "my name" (Jn 14:14, 15:16). That means praying about things that are in line with his agenda that we find in Scripture. The disciple of Christ should have prayer concerns that reflect God's heart.

Contributing to their spiritual deficiencies was their worldliness (4:4-5), which placed them in a position to receive God's judgment. It has often been stated that the contemporary church has become worldly, but what constitutes a worldly Christian? Is it having a glass of beer? Watching an R rated movie? Wearing a skirt four inches above the knee? Driving a Mercedes? To answer that question we need to go a little deeper in our understanding of what James means by worldly.

The Biblical definition of the "world" is organized society that leaves God out of the picture, making man the sole authority in defining truth, morality, ethics, worldview, and so forth.

One characteristic of our postmodern culture is that there are no absolute standards of truth, such that truth is relative to each individual, along with morality and ethics. In this type of environment the world says people should be accepting and tolerant of people who see things differently than you. Many believers have bought into this type of thinking and have adopted a posture which says that there are multiple pathways that lead to heaven; it could be through Buddha, Gandhi, Muhammad, or Jesus—take your pick! When believers adopt this value system, they have become worldly, because they are going against the clear teaching of Scripture.

Since the world says there are no absolute standards of truth, each individual creates his own version of morality, ethics, worldview, and so forth. Many believers will claim sex outside of marriage is an acceptable practice, over the clear teaching of Scripture that says it is not! Believers, under the banner of political correctness, will often be defenders of gay rights, and be advocates of same sex marriage, against the clear teaching of Scripture. When these values are adopted against the values set forth in Scripture, the believer has crossed the line and become worldly.

The things any culture produces that are contrary to God's standards such as: movies, music, literature, fashion, sitcoms, and whatever else is considered to be cool are a reflection of the world's system. When believers watch X rated movies, listen to music with lyrics that convey a message contrary to the Scripture, read the tabloid trash available at the grocery store, and embrace what culture says is in vogue, they have crossed the boundary line and are in worldly territory.

How does the believer keep himself spiritually viable in the midst of all the cultural influences that constantly bombard him? One solution is *isolation*: remove oneself from the world and join a monastery. Have nothing to do with the world whatsoever! That, however, makes fulfilling the Great Commission virtually impossible, so that isn't a good option!

Another option is **assimilation**, which also is not a good option. Assimilating worldly practices into your spiritual experience under the banner of tolerance and political correctness, only puts us in a bad place with God. This is the story of Israel! They assimilated into their own worship system the gods of the nations surrounding them. This brought God's judgment to bear on them, leading to the demise of their nation.

The best option is **insulation**. We live in the world everyday so we need to insulate ourselves against temptations and worldly sinful practices. We live in the world but are not of the world. In cold climates it's imperative to have a well insulated house to keep the cold out. In one's spiritual experience it is imperative to insulate oneself from worldly influences so we retain our purity. We insulate ourselves by having the word of God in our hearts (Ps 119:11), putting the armor on (Eph 6:10-18), and being filled with the Spirit (Eph 5:18)!

Obviously, God has a problem with worldliness! James has used harsh language by calling their worldliness spiritual adultery, hatred toward God, and even positioning themselves as an enemy of God. However, we would be remiss if we neglect to see the passion that God has for us. James uses the metaphor of the church being in a marriage relationship with the Lord. God is that jealous husband who desires the pure devotion of his bride (the church). He will not tolerate his bride committing adultery with the world system! One has to see the big heart of God who desires the pure devotion of his people, because he loves us! God's people often break his heart through their worldly behavior.

God understands, and gives us grace to compensate for our spiritual deficiencies, so we can be faithful to our Lord. This should bring us to a place of humility such that we seek God's grace, which empowers us to be faithful to him, and remain separate and distinct from the world! Without his enabling grace we will fail, for we can't do it on our own!

Chapter Thirteen

"The Solution to Conflict"

James 4:7-10

Submit yourselves, then, to God. Resist the devil, and he will flee from you. ⁸Come near to God and he will come near to you. Wash your hands, you sinners, and purify your hearts, you double-minded. ⁹Grieve, mourn and wail. Change your laughter to mourning and your joy to gloom. ¹⁰Humble yourselves before the Lord, and he will lift you up.

James has been describing a situation that is getting out of control! There is back-biting, favoritism, harsh language, spiritual adultery, and fights and quarrels in his congregation. It's not a pretty picture, so what can turn the situation around? This passage addresses the issue head on and is the heart of his homily. Repent! This Scripture serves as one of the most informative in the Bible about repentance, and does all believers well to spend some time here. Those who are behaving badly need to clean up their act by going through a thorough spiritual cleansing. They need to reposition themselves with God so that rather than having God oppose them, He will lift them up and give them grace. The way to do this is to obey the ten imperatives that James directs their way.

Submit yourselves, then, to God. Resist the devil, and he will flee from you. (4:7)

Repentance begins by reestablishing the Lordship of Christ in your life by submitting to God. Their lack of submission to God is portrayed by their worldliness, and walking in the wisdom from below, which stands in stark contrast to God's wisdom. The word submit (*hupotasso*) has military connotations. Literally it means to "arrange under." Troops would be arranged in formation under the command of their superior officer. In the military, soldiers understand the chain of command. You never disobey the orders of your superior office. Inherent in the command to submit, is the recognition that your superior has authority over you. Such is the case with the Lord Jesus! Each believer needs to acknowledge God's authority over his life. We are property of the Lord Jesus, for he has purchased us with his blood. The apostle Paul reminded the Corinthians of this when he said, "Do you not know that your bodies are temples of the Holy Spirit, who is in you, whom you have received from God? You are not your own; [20]you were bought at a price. Therefore honor God with your bodies (1 Cor 6:19-20)."

The people in James congregation that were behaving badly need to recognize the authority God has over them, and start following the orders of their commander-in-chief. They are spiritually going AWOL.

The other side of submitting to God is to resist the devil. Therefore, repentance is like two sides of a coin. One involves the believer's relationship to God, the other his relationship to the forces of darkness. Their drifting into the world, and committing spiritual adultery can be partly attributed to the influence of demonic forces, so James commands them to resist the devil. When Christians' behavior deteriorates as it did in James' congregations, somewhere in the picture Satan will be present. He was exerting his influence over those who were behaving badly. The fastest way to get rid of the enemy is to resist him. James doesn't tell us how to resist the enemy, he just gives the command. Resist is a translation of the Greek word *anthistemi,* and was used by Peter and Paul in their writings:

> **1 Peter 5:9:** Resist (*anthistemi*) him, standing firm in the faith, because you know that the family of believers throughout the world is undergoing the same kind of sufferings.

> **Ephesians 6:13:** Therefore put on the full armor of God, so that when the day of evil comes, you may be able to stand your ground (*anthistemi*), and after you have done everything, to stand.

It appears as though the devil is playing offense and the believers are on defense. The forces of darkness are on the attack, and believers need to hold their ground. Satan's strategies involve tempting God's people to sin! Given the behavior manifested by some in the congregation, the forces of darkness were having a degree of success. The false wisdom that the troublemakers displayed was described by James as earthly, unspiritual, and of the Devil (3:15). The bitter envy and selfish ambition that was driving some people can be attributed to the temptations of the enemy. When believers have the tendency to display vices characteristic of false wisdom, Satan can use his crafty influence on them, such that a multitude of expressions of evil can come to pass.

James was heavy on personal responsibility for sin, and was not quick to assign all human misconduct to the Devil (1:13-15), although the enemy probably has his fingers to a degree, in all human sinfulness. Under sever temptation one must be mindful of the faithfulness of God, in assisting the believer to overcome the assaults of the enemy. The apostle Paul reminded the Corinthians of this:

> No temptation has overtaken you except what is common to mankind. And God is faithful; he will not let you be tempted beyond what you can bear. But when you are tempted, he will also provide a way out so that you can endure it. (1 Cor 10:13)

Paul doesn't describe what the "way out" of a temptation is, nor did James describe how to resist the Devil. Common sense would indicate that disciples resist the Devil by trusting in the Lord moment-by-moment, and utilizing the resource of prayerful dependence on God. Additionally, all the weapons of the believers' warfare (2 Cor 10:3-5, Eph 6:10-18) can be brought to bear in the cosmic struggle God's people have against the forces of darkness, such as Scripture reading, worship, fellowship, obedience, and so forth.

When the devil is resisted he will flee. Although the evil one is powerful he isn't as powerful as we think, and quite often God's people give the Devil far more credit than he deserves. When temptations are resisted, the devil will leave us alone until he sees another opportune moment to continue the battle. He may return in 30 minutes, two hours, the next day, but be certain that he will show up again with another raging temptation to present to you. The believer must be vigilant, and constantly keep his spiritual guard up.

Come near to God and he will come near to you, (4:8a)

Coming near to God is virtually synonymous with the concept of worshiping God. When people approach God to worship him, they are said to come near or draw near to God (Heb 7:19, 10:1, 22). The expression "come near" was used of priests who minister before the Lord (Eze 44:15-16), and was also used as a call to worship (Ps 95). In the context at hand, it appears that the idea of drawing near to God carries with it the meaning expressed in Joel 2:12: "Even now,' declares the LORD, 'return to me with all your heart, with fasting and weeping and mourning."

In light of the impending judgment that was about to come on the Israelites, the prophet Joel admonished them to "return to me (God)" in the sense of repenting. In a similar way, James saw God's eschatological judgment as being imminent, and is admonishing the troublemakers to return to God in the sense of repenting and mending their errant ways.

It is implied that as the sinner draws near to God to worship him, that it is done with a sincere heart (Heb 10:22). Where true repentance exists, the disciple of Christ will want to be restored to fellowship with God, so the fractured relationship can be healed. God will reciprocate in kind by coming near to the sinner who repents. The rift can be healed as God restores the sinner! It is possible that the author had in mind Psalm 24:3-4 as he wrote verse eight:

> Who may ascend the mountain of the LORD? Who may stand in his holy place? [4]The one who has clean hands and a pure heart, who does not trust in an idol or swear by a false god.

Coming near to God, and standing in his holy place implies that repentance is genuine, resulting in holiness, obedience, performing good deeds, and walking in the wisdom from above. The "come near" language James uses reminds us of the covenant formula in Exodus 6:7: "I will take you as my own people, and I will be your God." There were stipulations in the covenant calling for obedience on behalf of God's people. When Israel drifted away from the Lord, he promised that when genuine repentance occurred he would offer forgiveness and restoration (2 Chro 7:14).

Wash your hands, you sinners, and purify your hearts, you double-minded, (4:8b)

As the priests in the Old Testament would come near to God to offer sacrifices in the tabernacle, they had to go through some elaborate rituals, one of which was a ceremonial washing of the hands and feet (Ex 30:18-21, Lev 16:4). This symbolically represented washing the sin out of their lives. Having clean hands before the Lord was synonymous with living a pure life. In one of David's Psalms he said: "The LORD has dealt with me according to my righteousness; according to the cleanness of my hands he has rewarded me (Psalm 18:20)." Obviously, David's clean hands indicate a life that is submitted to God and bearing fruit. When the Lord chastised his people through the prophet Isaiah he said:

> When you spread out your hands in prayer, I hide my eyes from you; even when you offer many prayers, I am not listening. Your hands are full of blood! 16Wash and make yourselves clean. Take your evil deeds out of my sight; stop doing wrong. 17Learn to do right; seek justice. Defend the oppressed. Take up the cause of the

> fatherless; plead the case of the widow. (Isaiah
> 1:15-17)

In essence, James is challenging the people to clean up their spiritual act! He pulls no punches by calling them sinners. Through the symbolism of washing their hands, James is telling them they need to use a little bit of soap and water on their lives, and remove the filth of sin. Next, James directs the attention of the people inward to the heart—for sin is always a matter of the heart! Commenting on the corrupt nature of the human heart Jesus said:

> But the things that come out of a person's mouth
> come from the heart, and these defile them. [19]For
> out of the heart come evil thoughts—murder,
> adultery, sexual immorality, theft, false testimony,
> slander. (Matthew 15:18-19)

No believer will ever be perfectly pure in heart because of the corruption inherent in fallen humanity. The point James is making is that "clean hands" connote good deeds while the "pure heart" connotes the inward disposition of a heart that is submitted to God. Thus, James deals with external behavior and the inner condition of the heart in his call to repentance. That James calls them double-minded indicates that they were conflicted! Their loyalties were divided between walking in the world, and walking with God. James already used the term double-minded to describe the man whose prayer life is characterized by vacillating between faith and doubt (1:8). In the present verse, James is describing the man who is thoroughly torn between the world, and faithfulness to God. The solution to the problem is to purify the heart, by having a single-minded allegiance to God. No more divided loyalties!

Grieve, mourn and wail. Change your laughter to mourning and your joy to gloom, (4:9)

The three words form a triplet, fitting nicely together as a description of the emotional response of the sinner who repents before God. When someone is truly cognizant of their sinfulness, there will be an accompanying grief or sorrow that they feel regarding their spiritual condition. Speaking through the prophet Joel, God told his people "to return to me with all your heart, with fasting and weeping and mourning; rend your heart, and not your garments (Joel 2:12-13a)."

The apostle Paul established one of the benchmarks of true repentance as being godly sorrow that brings repentance that leads to salvation…(2 Cor 7:10). He called for the Corinthians to grieve over a terrible act of sin committed in their church (1 Cor 5:2). When Peter betrayed Jesus by denying him three times, Peter wept (Mark 14:72), which was an expression of his sorrow for his actions. When a believer's life has become overrun by sin, repentance will be accompanied by some painful remorse over their spiritual condition. Failure of this to happen calls into question the genuineness one's repentance.

James is not advocating that Christians live a lifestyle that is free of laughter and joy. In the context of repentance, he is suggesting that Christians adopt a different attitude about life. Rather than going through life in a carefree manner—adopting the philosophy of "eat, drink and be merry", "go for the gusto", or "party hardy", James is calling for an attitude that takes God seriously. The one who goes through life "laughing" is the one who lives for the pleasures of this world, and ignores the reality of God's imminent judgment. Believers can become desensitized to sin and need to repent of their hedonistic tendencies (4:3) and stop having an affair with the world (4:4).

The believer who turns his laughter to mourning as he repents of sin, is showing evidence of his genuine repentance.

The Lord Jesus spoke about the contrast of values between those in the world and those who choose the life of discipleship. In Luke 6:21b he said, "Blessed are you who weep now, for you will laugh." Believers who weep over their sinfulness now, will experience laughter and joy when God settles accounts on judgment day. To those who adopt the values of the world system Jesus said, "Woe to you who laugh now, for you will mourn and weep (Luke 6:25b)." These people will experience the terrifying nature of God's judgment, and will mourn and weep as never before.

Joy is a normal part of the believer's experience of knowing Christ, and is a fruit of the Spirit (Gal 5:22). Turning your joy into gloom is another way of saying turn your laughter to mourning. The world's joy is superficial and fleeting. True laughter and joy will be found only after true repentance occurs. The believer can only know the joy of the Lord as he honestly deals with his sin!

Humble yourselves before the Lord, and he will lift you up. (4:10)

This verse takes us back to verse six, where James introduced the theme of humility before God as the pathway to experience his grace. Now James returns to the theme of humility as the means to experience God's exaltation. Therefore, vv. 6 and 10 are like bookends on each side of the ten commands for repentance (vv. 7-9). Humility is the starting point of repentance before God, and should be a constant in our walk with the Lord. Being humble before the Lord requires an attitude of dependence, submission, and seeking the Lord's strength to help us overcome our own sinful tendencies.

Those who humble themselves before the Lord will be rewarded. He will give grace and lift up those with humble hearts. Jesus said: "For all those who exalt themselves will be humbled, and those who humble themselves will be exalted." (Luke 18:14b)

The trouble-makers who are driven by their bitter envy and selfish ambition as they try to make a name for themselves, will be humbled by God's judgment. They need to humble themselves before the Lord, and position themselves so they receive his grace and his exaltation. The place of exaltation, that God will bring the repentant sinner, is a place where he is living correctly before the Lord, enjoying his blessings, controlling his mouth, letting go of his hedonistic tendencies, and doing good works done with gentleness that comes from wisdom (3:13). James' call to humility should remind us of the importance of banishing pride from our thoughts, and remind us of what a grace-killer self-exaltation can be. We end this section with a reminder from God himself that he favors those who are humble:

> For this is what the high and exalted One says—
> he who lives forever, whose name is holy: "I live
> in a high and holy place, but also with the one
> who is contrite and lowly in spirit, to revive the
> spirit of the lowly and to revive the heart of the
> contrite. (Isaiah 57:15).

Insights and Application, (4:7-10)

When things deteriorate to the point where God's people are behaving badly and are out of control, you can bet that Satan is somewhere in the mix. The first thing that James tells his people to do is "Submit yourselves then, to God, and resist the Devil." The wisdom from below (3:13-18) always results in division, mass chaos, and fractured relationships. You can bet that Satan is all over that! That is the effect of his presence in the midst of God's people.

Where there is strife and contention among God's people we can't be ignorant of the Devil's schemes. Often times we don't give the Devil enough credit, and sometimes we give him too much credit. There are those who so minimize the work of Satan that they never even consider his presence or contribution to a divisive situation. Then, there are those who see Satan behind every pew in the sanctuary, attributing everything to him including the car breaking down, the kids getting sick, and the feedback in the sound system during the worship on Sunday morning.

It is wise to have a balanced view of Satan and his minions. Let's give him the credit that one would give a worthy adversary, and let's not become obsessed with him such that we think more about Satan than we do God. Spiritual warfare is a normal part of the everyday experience of a believer.

From reading Ephesians 6:10-18, it should be obvious that Paul considered Satan a worthy opponent that the believer must take seriously:

> Finally, be strong in the Lord and in his mighty power. [11]Put on the full armor of God, so that you can take your stand against the devil's schemes. [12]For our struggle is not against flesh and blood, but against the rulers, against the authorities, against the powers of this dark world and against the spiritual forces of evil in the heavenly realms. [13]Therefore put on the full armor of God, so that when the day of evil comes, you may be able to stand your ground, and after you have done

everything, to stand. [14]Stand firm then, with the belt of truth buckled around your waist, with the breastplate of righteousness in place, [15]and with your feet fitted with the readiness that comes from the gospel of peace. [16]In addition to all this, take up the shield of faith, with which you can extinguish all the flaming arrows of the evil one. [17]Take the helmet of salvation and the sword of the Spirit, which is the word of God. [18]And pray in the Spirit on all occasions with all kinds of prayers and requests. With this in mind, be alert and always keep on praying for all the Lord's people.

Paul imagines a Roman soldier putting on all his gear, getting suited up for battle. He applies this to the Christian getting suited up for battle against the forces of darkness. God's people need to be combat ready in their everyday experience because Satan is at war with us! We better take this seriously! On the other hand, Satan is a defeated foe at the cross, we have victory over him in Christ—his destiny is eternity in the lake of fire. We have authority over the evil one, so we need to make sure we don't give him more credit than he deserves.

Repentance is a buzzword in the Christian community, however we rarely see it happen the way James describes it. Washing your hands, purifying your heart, eliminating double-mindedness all points the repentant one in the direction of transformation. True repentance does lead to a changed life. The following passages reveal the relationship between repentance and behavioral change:

Acts 26:20: First to those in Damascus, then to those in Jerusalem and in all Judea, and then to the Gentiles, I preached that they should repent and turn to God and demonstrate their repentance by their deeds.

Mat 3:6-8: Confessing their sins, they were baptized by him in the Jordan River. [7]But when he saw many of the Pharisees and Sadducees coming to where he was baptizing, he said to them: "You brood of vipers! Who warned you to flee from the coming wrath? [8]Produce fruit in keeping with repentance.

2 Cor 7:9-10: yet now I am happy, not because you were made sorry, but because your sorrow led you to repentance. For you became sorrowful as God intended and so were not harmed in any way by us. [10]Godly sorrow brings repentance that leads to salvation and leaves no regret, but worldly sorrow brings death.

If someone claims to have repented of their sins, but no evidence of that exists in their daily behavior, one has to conclude that their repentance is highly suspect!

Repentance can be emotionally taxing, at times even gut-wrenching! Depending on the gravity of the sin(s), it can be an emotionally draining experience. Consider the following passages:

Jeremiah 6:26: Put on sackcloth, my people, and roll in ashes; mourn with bitter wailing as for an only son, for suddenly the destroyer will come upon us.

Jeremiah 4:8: So put on sackcloth, lament and wail, for the fierce anger of the Lord has not turned away from us.

Esther 4:1-3: When Mordecai learned of all that had been done, he tore his clothes, put on sackcloth and ashes, and went out into the city, wailing loudly and bitterly. ²But he went only as far as the king's gate, because no one clothed in sackcloth was allowed to enter it. ³In every province to which the edict and order of the king came, there was great mourning among the Jews, with fasting, weeping and wailing. Many lay in sackcloth and ashes.

Ezra 9:3-6: When I heard this, I tore my tunic and cloak, pulled hair from my head and beard and sat down appalled. ⁴Then everyone who trembled at the words of the God of Israel gathered around me because of this unfaithfulness of the exiles. And I sat there appalled until the evening sacrifice. ⁵Then, at the evening sacrifice, I rose from my self-abasement, with my tunic and cloak torn, and fell on my knees with my hands spread out to the LORD my God ⁶and prayed: "I am too ashamed and disgraced, my God, to lift up my face to you, because our sins are higher than our heads and our guilt has reached to the heavens.

Becoming fully aware of the gravity of our own sinfulness can be painful! When someone repents of sin while watching the game on TV, eating a bag of potato chips, and drinking a cold brew, one has to question the seriousness of the repentance.

Chapter Fourteen

"Do Not Speak Against Your Brother"

James 4:11-12

Brothers and sisters, do not slander one another. Anyone who speaks against a brother or sister or judges them speaks against the law and judges it. When you judge the law, you are not keeping it, but sitting in judgment on it. ¹²There is only one Lawgiver and Judge, the one who is able to save and destroy. But you—who are you to judge your neighbor?

It seems as though there is an abrupt change in the topic, with little or no connection to the previous section. However, James has said much about sins of the tongue (3:1-12) and this may be his summary statement of the problem of sinful communication. Another possible link with the previous section is that after James discussed repentance and restoration with God, he now turns to the horizontal dimension and encourages proper treatment of those in the body of Christ regarding their communication. This reminds us of the first and second commands as stated by the Lord Jesus—loving God and then loving your neighbor as yourself (Mat 22:37-39). True repentance involves the vertical dimension with God, but has to include the horizontal plane with your fellow man.

Brothers and sisters, do not slander one another. Anyone who speaks against a brother or sister or judges them speaks against the law and judges it. When you judge the law, you are not keeping it, but sitting in judgment on it. (4:11)

Once again, James uses the endearing term "brothers and sisters" to remind them of the familial nature of the body of Christ, and show his tender pastoral heart. That brothers in Christ slander and speak against each other makes the matter all the more flagrant! Brothers in the Lord should not treat each other that way. Slander translates the Greek word *katalaleo,* which includes a wide variety of verbal infractions, including gossiping about someone, backbiting, defamation of character, making false accusations, speaking unkindly about people, saying things of a derogatory nature, and so forth. As James penned this section he may have had been drawing from Leviticus 19:16a which says: "Do not go about spreading slander among your people." This activity is totally uncalled for among God's people! Brothers in Christ should use their verbal skills to build one another up, rather than tearing each other down!

Another verbal sin James mentions is judging your brother. This sin involves standing above your brother nit-picking him, fault-finding, and being hyper-critical of him. In doing this the guilty party is heaping guilt, condemnation, and punishment on his brother that Jesus died for! This form of judging is forbidden because it is only God's place to judge others. Jesus addressed the issue of hypocrisy in standing in judgment of people in the Sermon on the Mount where he said:

"Do not judge, or you too will be judged. [2]For in the same way you judge others, you will be judged, and with the measure you use, it will be measured to you. [3]"Why do you look at the speck of sawdust in your brother's eye and pay no attention to the plank in your own eye? [4]How can you say to your brother, 'Let me take the speck out of your eye,' when all the time there is a plank in your own eye? [5]You hypocrite, first take the plank out of your own eye, and then you will see clearly to remove the speck from your brother's eye." (Matthew 7:1-5)

Often we are guilty of the very thing we see in our brother, but to a greater degree! We have the proverbial blind spot and are oblivious to the plank in our own eye, while we get in our brother's face over the speck in his eye. It isn't wrong to call a brother on a sin! We do him a service by exercising accountability and offering a word of admonishment. The key is in the manner that we approach our brother. When I admonish a brother, I stand beside him and encourage him in love, to "raise the bar" for the Lord. When I judge my brother, I stand above him and discourage him through condemnation, with no love in my heart! The result is that I make myself out to be a hypocrite, and I most likely sever my relationship with the brother I just wounded.

Another reason why speaking against and judging our brothers is taboo, is that when we do so, we "speak against the law and judge it". Keeping the law is of vital importance for Jews; for nobody would want to be a lawbreaker. James had made references to the law several times (1:25, 2:8, 12). The ninth commandment is "You shall not give false testimony against your neighbor (Exodus 20:16)." With all the mud-slinging going on, this part of the law was being grossly violated (cf Lev

19:16a). The law of love that Jesus instituted regarding loving your neighbor as yourself (Mat 22:39, Lev 19:18), was also being disregarded through the verbal thrashing that was taking place. By violating the law, James considers this the equivalent of speaking against the law and passing judgment on it as well. The violator disregards the authority of the law, thus standing in judgment over it.

This assumes that James readers knew the law, but willfully disregarded it. Believers don't have the option of choosing which commands of Scripture they want to obey and which they choose to ignore. When Christians deliberately chose to ignore a portion of the law, they show an arrogant attitude of superiority over the law, which James considers judging the law. James will have none of that!

There is only one Lawgiver and Judge, the one who is able to save and destroy. But you—who are you to judge your neighbor? (4:12)

The law originated with God and was given to the people to instruct them how to live, so they could maximize God's blessings in their lives. His Word is truth and was to be obeyed. Their obedience would bring them blessings, whereas their disobedience would have dire consequences. Only God occupies the unique role of giving the law and judging people on the basis of their adherence to the same.

The Lawgiver and Judge is also the only one who is able to save and destroy. James echoes the words of Jesus: "Do not be afraid of those who kill the body but cannot kill the soul. Rather, be afraid of the One who can destroy both soul and body in hell (Matthew 10:28)." The ultimate judgment is life or death, salvation or destruction. Only God can make those kinds of judgments, because in his omniscience he can peer into the depths of the human heart and see faith or lack thereof (Heb 4:12-13).

Perhaps, some people were judging others by accusing them of not being true believers in Christ. James' response to them is "but you—who are you to judge your neighbor?" By judging their neighbor they bring themselves into a position to be judged by the One who has the power of life and death, salvation or destruction. This should serve as a word of caution and give the guilty parties something to think about. Previously, James said "because judgment without mercy will be shown to anyone who has not been merciful. Mercy triumphs over judgment (2:13)!" In addition to the love ethic taught by Jesus, the Lord saw mercy as a vital expression of faith. The verbal sins in the community were a gross violation of the love and mercy ethic that should be inherent in the Christian life.

The heart of the law according to Jesus, was to love the Lord and your neighbor as yourself (Mat 22:37-39, Lev 19:18). How much more should we love those who are fellow believers in Christ. The guilty parties have crossed the line with God and are infringing on his exclusive right to judge, while they are breaking Jesus' royal law: love your neighbor as yourself (2:8). Those who do this show no evidence of repentance and submission to God (4:7).

Insights and Application, (4:11-12)

This brief passage should have a sobering effect on the reader. We are all guilty of judging people and being overly critical of those with whom we worship. The world would be a kinder and gentler place if everybody could put this Scripture into practice.

Before I speak against, or stand in judgment of a brother in Christ, I better make sure I'm not guilty of the same thing(s) about which I'm going to confront my brother. If I go to straighten out my brother regarding sin in his life, but I have the same sin in mine, I make myself out to be a hypocrite—I have a double standard! It's not OK for my brother to do it, but it's all right for me to do it. In fact, I may be more guilty than my brother regarding the sin I'm calling him on, and not even be aware of it. Hence, the need exits to go through a reality check about myself before I go to my brother to correct him about a sin in his life. If I determine I have the same behavior in my life that I'm finding unacceptable in my brother, I have no business going to my brother and blasting him! I need to deal with my own issues first.

Everybody needs to recognize the responsibility we have to hold one another accountable in a spirit of love. For instance, I have friends in my life that will call me to the carpet if they see me being less than what I should be in the Lord. These same friends would also expect me to inform them if I see them beginning to slip in their walk with Christ. My wife is my front line of accountability in my home, in the church the elders serve that purpose, and beyond that I have friends I hang out with that will let me know when I need to tighten things up for the Lord. When someone comes to me in a loving manner and confronts me on something in my life, that isn't being judgmental, or speaking against me in a slanderous way. That person is doing me a service in the Lord!

Often times people will see a brother slipping in his walk with the Lord, but nobody says anything to him for fear that they might hurt his feelings, offend him, or even start a fight. By saying nothing they do the brother a grave disservice, and allow him to continue on in his dysfunction! Often times an intervention, although it can be painful, can steer someone from a harmful path and turn his life around. To avoid an intervention because you lack the courage, or fear hurting his feelings is unacceptable. God may be using you to speak into that brother's life and bring him to his spiritual senses, but you don't want to answer the call! You fail the Lord and your brother!

James isn't saying that all judging is wrong. There are times when judging one's behavior is totally appropriate and necessary. For example, when selecting people for church leadership to occupy positions like elder, deacons, teachers, and so on, there has to be good discernment exercised in evaluating the person under consideration for the positions. Scripture does set forth a number of criteria that must be satisfied in order to occupy certain offices in the church. It is entirely responsible for the leaders of a church to evaluate a person's life to see if they are qualified to be in leadership. This isn't fault-finding, and back-biting that James is talking about.

We also are called to exercise good discernment regarding whom we choose to become good friends with. This isn't nit-picking and being judgmental like James is talking about. Wisdom is necessary in choosing those we let into our inner circle, and place our trust in. Having positive influences in our lives helps us grow in the Lord, while the negative influencers can prove to be harmful to our spiritual experience.

Paul once told the Corinthians that we shouldn't judge those outside the church, but rather those inside the church should be the object of judgment (1 Cor 5:1-5). There was a grave matter of sin that was committed in the church and the membership laughed about it, like it was the latest and greatest joke. Paul demanded that they judge the man and expel him from the congregation because the sin was so reprehensible that even the pagans didn't do things of that nature. Matters of church discipline can't be overlooked because we are afraid it might appear that we are being judgmental.

Believers have no right to hold nonbelievers to the same standards by which believers are obligated to live. Nonbelievers have an entirely different worldview that stands at odds with the Christian worldview. We damage our opportunities to witness for Christ when we stand in judgment of those who don't know the Lord.

Chapter Fifteen

"Submitting Our Plans To God"

James 4:13-17

Now listen, you who say, "Today or tomorrow we will go to this or that city, spend a year there, carry on business and make money." ¹⁴Why, you do not even know what will happen tomorrow. What is your life? You are a mist that appears for a little while and then vanishes. ¹⁵Instead, you ought to say, "If it is the Lord's will, we will live and do this or that." ¹⁶As it is, you boast in your arrogant schemes. All such boasting is evil. ¹⁷If anyone, then, knows the good they ought to do and doesn't do it, it is sin for them.

It wasn't uncommon for merchants to travel a great deal before they could settle down in Palestine. Those who have an entrepreneurial spirit, and make plans to do business in various cities need to take into consideration God's will as they map out their future. Thinking we can plot the course of our life independently of God is prideful and indicates a lack of submission to his will. We have no control over the variables of life, not even knowing what could happen tomorrow. Given these limitations on the human experience, James now discusses how the believer should submit their plans to God.

Now listen, you who say, "Today or tomorrow we will go to this or that city, spend a year there, carry on business and make money." (4:13)

James is trying to get their attention, so he begins by saying the equivalent of "Pay attention" or "Listen Up." This may sound a bit harsh, so why would James address his readers in this way? When one reads verse 13 there is no sin to be found. These merchants are putting together a business plan, which is what any entrepreneur should do! They are identifying the following things in their business plan: 1) the time of their venture is "today or tomorrow", 2) the location is "this or that city", 3) the duration is "spend a year there", 4) the activity is to "carry on business", and 5) the purpose is to "make money". This sounds like it has the making of an effective business proposal, and they should be commended for planning everything out! There is no sin specifically mentioned, but one has to wonder if they've prayed about it? Did they consult God about their plans? Did they feel that God was leading them in this direction? It appears not, and there lies their sin!

Why, you do not even know what will happen tomorrow. What is your life? You are a mist that appears for a little while and then vanishes. (4:14)

One problem with trying to map out your future—is that the future is out of your control. There are so many variables in life that we have no control over, such that thinking one can successfully plan out every detail of your life is foolishness and prideful. Today may be a good day, but tomorrow I could contract a serious illness, the stock market could crash, a war could begin, and so forth. Only God has control over these things! When writing this verse James may have had Proverbs 27:1 in mind, which says "Do not boast about tomorrow, for you do not know what a day may bring." Every believer needs to have a balance of planning things out, but leaving room for the possibility that the unexpected may happen, resulting in altering the plans we were certain of.

James provides a second reason why trying to map out your future independently of consulting God is an attempt in futility: "What is your life"? James brings to our attention the brevity of human existence—"you are a mist that appears and then vanishes." In the grand scheme of eternity the seventy or eighty years one may spend on earth is like a mist that is here and gone in a heartbeat. Given the brevity of human life, and the fact that we could literally be here today and gone tomorrow, should cause the believer to focus his attention on living for God every moment! Time is a valuable commodity, but it is running out for every person, so the wisest use of time is making sure we are dialed into God moment-by-moment!

Instead, you ought to say, "If it is the Lord's will, we will live and do this or that." ¹⁶As it is, you boast in your arrogant schemes. All such boasting is evil. (4:15-16)

Where the merchants made their mistake—was in not discerning what God's will was for them in making their ambitious plans. In trying to discern God's will it is assumed that they would invest some time in praying about their plans, seeking the Lord's wisdom for their situation (1:5), consulting the Scriptures for guidance, and getting some feedback from other mature Christians (Pro 15:22). None of this happened! God was completely bypassed in making their plans. One insightful passage to be considered by those who are making plans for the future is Proverbs 16:1-3:

> To humans belong the plans of the heart, but
> from the LORD comes the proper answer of the
> tongue. ²All a person's ways seem pure to them,
> but motives are weighed by the LORD. ³Commit to
> the LORD whatever you do, and he will establish
> your plans.

James implies that the scope of the Lord's will is exhaustive! If it is the Lord's will "we will live." Life itself is within the grasp of God's will as the giver, sustainer, and taker of life. "Doing this or that" pertaining to whatever activities one engages in, should illicit a sense of humble dependence upon the Lord.

Rather than seeking the Lord in their planning they are guilty of boasting and bragging, "and all such boasting is evil"! In what sense were they boasting? Their prideful boasting was reflected in the fact that they thought they could plan out their future and control all the variables without consulting God. This type of mindset is reflected in one of Jesus' parables where he described a man who devised a brilliant plan to go into early retirement. He had amassed enough goods so he could kick back, take it easy, and enjoy life. However, the unexpected happened: "But God said to him, 'You fool! This very night your life will be demanded from you. Then who will get what you have prepared for yourself (Luke 12:20)?" He thought he had it all figured out, but he became painfully aware that his time was up, and his moment of death was at hand! Perhaps it was the unexpected heart attack, aggressive cancer, or some other malady that claimed his life. This parable points out the folly of omitting God from our planning. James considers this approach to life to be evil!

If anyone, then, knows the good they ought to do and doesn't do it, it is sin for them. (4:17)

Sins of commission are those things we knowingly do that are displeasing to God. Sins of omission are those things we know that we are supposed to do, but fail to do, hence, the term omission. James made reference to a situation where a brother did nothing to help someone who needed food and clothing (2:15-16), except to wish them well! Their faith should have moved them to lend a helping hand to the brother in need. Not coming to the aid of this needy brother is a sin of omission!

Christians know they should be prayerful and consult God regarding their plans for the future, but often don't bother. This is sinful, and if we back up to verse 16, it could be considered outright evil! Christian businessmen, or Christians in general, who are presumptuously boasting about their successes and ingenious planning abilities, without including God in the picture, are guilty of committing a heinous sin in the eyes of God. In essence, they are living like atheists! They may profess belief in God, be born again, and truly know the Lord Jesus, but in their daily decision-making they live like atheists. They have a minimal awareness of the presence of Christ in their life, which minimizes his Lordship over them.

Insights and Application, (4:13-17)

All believers need to be good stewards by planning for retirement, saving for their kid's college education, and living within their means, but at the same time the possibility for the unexpected is always present. Thus, a tension exists between being good planners, and having incomplete control over your plans. That is the nature of human existence! We may be navigating a well-devised course for our lives, but God could intervene and change the plan for us like he did with Jonah. God showed up one day and had an assignment for him that he didn't like, such that he actually ran away from the Lord, trying to get out of it. God, however, wouldn't let him off the hook!

We could be staying on course following our plans for the future, but the economy could go into recession, the stock market could crash and our plans for the future need to be revised. Our life may be going along very well, according to plan, but you get cancer and everything changes. Your plans for the future need to be rethought. Therefore, every believer needs to make plans and practice good stewardship, but acknowledge that the possibility of something happening (an act of God) could wipe out your well-thought-out plans.

The most frequently asked question that I've had people propose to me in pastoral counseling is: "How can I know what God's will is for this season of my life?" When people have a major life-impacting decision to make, of extreme importance to them is knowing what God would have them do! How does the believer discern God's will?

There are several things that Christians can do to discern God's will for a given situation listed below.

#1. What are the motives behind the decision, or the course of action you're considering? Is this something that you feel the Lord is leading you in, or is this something that is selfishly motivated that you've dreamed up? Sometimes we have to search our hearts to gain clarity why we are considering a course of action. The passage from Proverbs 16:1-3 speaks to the disciple who is making some plans for his future:

> To humans belong the plans of the heart, but from the LORD comes the proper answer of the tongue. ²All a person's ways seem pure to them, but motives are weighed by the LORD. ³Commit to

the LORD whatever you do, and he will establish your plans.

Of importance is verse two, which informs us that motives are weighed by the Lord, which indicates that one's motives can be suspect. There are a variety of influences in a person's life that can steer one to make a bad decision including peer pressure, one's own sinful desires, influence from the demonic realm, and so forth. Try to gain understanding regarding the purity of your motives in making a particular decision.

#2. Always consult God's word for guidance and make sure that whatever decision is being considered isn't in violation of God's Word. This might seem very obvious, but in my experience it is not uncommon for people to know what the clear teaching of Scripture is, but go against it anyway! It happens all the time! Believers shack up rather than getting married, they have sex outside of marriage, get in debt up to their eyeballs, knowing full-well their choices go against the Scripture. Psalm 119:24 says: "Your statutes are my delight; they are my counselors." Listen to the counsel of God's word.

#3. Always devote yourself to prayer when making a critical decision in life. The apostle Paul said in 1 Thess 5:17: "pray continually." Regular prayer is one of the most vital parts of discerning God's will for your life. James has informed his readers in 1:5: "If any of you lacks wisdom, he should ask God, who gives generously to all without finding fault, and it will be given to him." This is a great promise for disciples who are seeking wisdom from on high, when sorting through different options in their decision making. In those stressful times when one considers major life transitions, it is comforting to know that God will impart wisdom when we ask for it. He won't hang us out to dry!

#4. In any major decision in life it is always beneficial to get counsel from some mature Christians that you know and trust. Proverbs 15:22 sheds some light on the importance of getting feedback before a critical decision is made: "Plans fail for lack of counsel, but with many advisers they succeed." We all have blind spots! A trusted brother in the Lord who will give you honest input can be a valuable resource in helping you make the right decision, that leads you away from failure and into success.

#5. In any undertaking, it is necessary to consider your level of skill. I once knew a person who was working on his undergraduate degree with the intentions of going to medical school. His problem was that he wasn't a very good student! He would enroll for a full load of classes every semester (21 credits worth). As the semester was drawing to a close, whatever classes became apparent that he wasn't going to get an A, he would drop and take them the next time they were offered. Every semester he dropped several classes, and was going at a snail's pace through school. He finally realized that at the rate he was going, by the time he got into med school, he would be in his forties! He came to the conclusion that he didn't have the level of skill necessary to make it in medical school, so he became a nurse and did very well.

#6. Circumstances often point you in the direction of God's will. On one occasion Paul was in Troas, and based on the circumstances that presented themselves he concluded he was right where he was supposed to be: "Now when I went to Troas to preach the gospel of Christ and found that the Lord had opened a door for me...(2 Cor 2:12)." Paul was in Troas preaching the gospel and people got saved! He concluded that the Lord had opened this door for him, which led to the foundation of a new church in that city. Paul concluded through his circumstances that the Lord opened a door for him, leading him to believe that he was right where God wanted him to be.

Recently some high school graduates in my church were submitting their applications to various colleges, not being sure of where God wanted them to go. God made things easy for one student to discern his will, because of the three colleges he applied to, two letters of rejection preceded the one letter of acceptance. The circumstances that prevailed led the student to understand that God pointed him in the direction of that particular college. Often times the Lord speaks to us through open or closed doors.

#7. Whenever facing major decisions in life, always count the cost before making the decision. On one occasion Jesus addressed the cost of discipleship and said:

> "Suppose one of you wants to build a tower. Won't you first sit down and estimate the cost to see if you have enough money to complete it? 29For if you lay the foundation and are not able to finish it, everyone who sees it will ridicule you, 30saying, 'This person began to build and wasn't able to finish.' 31"Or suppose a king is about to go to war against another king. Won't he first sit down and consider whether he is able with ten thousand men to oppose the one coming against him with twenty thousand? 32If he is not able, he will send a delegation while the other is still a long way off and will ask for terms of peace. 33In the same way, those of you who do not give up everything you have cannot be my disciples. (Luke 14:28-33)

Jesus was making the point that there is a cost to becoming one of his followers. That cost must be carefully considered before making the decision to become his disciple. In the above illustration, the builder will be considered foolish if he can't complete the building he started because he didn't plan it correctly. The King going to war will be defeated in battle if he doesn't first determine that he has the ability to defeat his opponent.

Likewise, before you plot a course in life make sure you have the resources available to complete the task. If you're thinking of returning to school and working on a Master's degree, can your kids handle not spending as much time with you as before? Is there enough money available to pay for tuition? Is your husband supportive of your effort? Do you have the emotional and mental fortitude to complete the task? If the answer is "no" to the above questions, perhaps it's not the time to go back to school.

#8. Lastly, a sense of inner peace can bring validation to a divinely directed course of action. When you've done all the things listed above, do you have a sense of peace about your plans, or are you disturbed about them? God will give us a sense of peace when leading us down a path. Paul mentioned the peace of God which surpasses all understanding in Philippians 4:7, which he experienced when he was in prison. God's peace accompanies God's will.

The above steps will help you determine God's will for any season of your life. When we charge ahead with our plans without consulting God, we are living like we are atheists! We may be born again, saved by the blood of Jesus, but in everyday affairs we live like nonbelievers, and do our own thing! Such is the case with believers who plan independently of consulting God.

CHAPTER SIXTEEN

"JUDGMENT IS IMMANENT"

James 5:1-6

Now listen, you rich people, weep and wail because of the misery that is coming on you. ²Your wealth has rotted, and moths have eaten your clothes. ³Your gold and silver are corroded. Their corrosion will testify against you and eat your flesh like fire. You have hoarded wealth in the last days. ⁴Look! The wages you failed to pay the workers who mowed your fields are crying out against you. The cries of the harvesters have reached the ears of the Lord Almighty. ⁵You have lived on earth in luxury and self-indulgence. You have fattened yourselves in the day of slaughter. ⁶You have condemned and murdered the innocent one, who was not opposing you.

James has said a great deal about money in his homily (1:9-12, 2:1-7, 4:13-17). In order to properly understand this section we need to ascertain the identity of the rich people being addressed. It is certainly a group other than the Christian businessmen that James spoke to in 4:13-17. In this section,

James is speaking to nonbelievers that were filthy rich, were guilty of gross mismanagement of their goods, and other sinful practices, such that they had positioned themselves to receive God's judgment. These wealthy landowners often stole the land out from under the feet of the poor, then hired them as day laborers, paying them practically nothing for their work. James frames God's impending judgment upon these wealthy people in an eschatological perspective—they have hoarded wealth in the last days. It appears that James understands God's judgment as being immanent.

There were wealthy landowners who became more wealthy and corrupt. Many people in James' congregation suffered at their hands, and making things more difficult, some of the wealthy people may have been attending their gatherings periodically, even though they weren't born again Christians. It may be possible, that some of them later became believers and needed to clean up their act, and cease their detestable practices!

In language reminiscent of Old Testament prophets, James has some tough words for them that need to be taken seriously! As this letter was read out loud to the people, if the rich were in attendance, it would certainly get their attention! For the rest of the believers, and especially those suffering at the hands of the rich, they would be encouraged to know that God sees their suffering, and the injustices taking place. Even more, God is going to do something about it. In the end, things won't work out very well for the rich people, because God will intervene and make things right!

Now listen, you rich people, weep and wail because of the misery that is coming upon you. (5:1)

James uses the same address he used in verse 13 to get their attention. Although things may be going quite well for the rich in the present, their future isn't looking very bright. James instructs them to weep and wail because of the impending disaster that is coming upon them. In the prophets, weeping and wailing are emotions associated with the reaction of the wicked when the day of the Lord arrives (Isa 13:6, 15:3, 16:7, 23:1, Jer 2:23, 31:20, Eze 21:17, Amos 8:3, Hos 7:14, Zech 11:2). Weep translates the Greek word *klaio* and refers to an intense sobbing or lamenting. Wail is a translation of *ololuzo* which connotes shrieking, crying out in grief, or screaming.

These two words taken together present a graphic, and rather sad, picture of nonbelievers crying out in pain, like a wounded beast in the forest as they receive God's judgment. The word misery (*talaiporia*) is actually plural, which intensifies the degree of suffering that they will experience when God intervenes. The word carries the idea of hardship, trouble and calamity.

Your wealth has rotted, and moths have eaten your clothes. ³Your gold and silver are corroded. Their corrosion will testify against you and eat your flesh like fire. You have hoarded wealth in the last days. (5:2-3)

James will now enumerate the sins of the rich that are bringing God's judgment upon them. That their wealth has rotted would seem to be a reference to agricultural products such as grain, meat, oil and other goods. They had amassed so many goods that they couldn't possibly use them so they spoiled. In a world where food was hard to come by, and for most people was in short supply, their hoarding is a massive insult to the poor who could have benefited from their excess.

They had so many clothes that their closets were bursting at the seams! In the ancient world clothes and jewelry were status symbols and reflections of a person's wealth. The impression given by James is that they had so many clothes that they couldn't possibly use them, so the moths got the best of them. In those days the average person had one garment. Clothes were a great luxury, and rather than giving their excess clothing away so that somebody else could use them, they rotted in their closets. Another insult to the poor and needy!

The next item James mentions is precious metals—gold and silver, which are corroding. The difficulty here is that gold and silver don't corrode or rust, but they do tarnish and need to be polished. Some coins in that era weren't made of pure silver or gold and were known to rust. Perhaps, James uses the word in the general sense of decay.

James uses the perfect tense in Greek, which suggests that the goods being hoarded are already in the state of being rotted, eaten by moths, and rusting. The picture James paints of these wealthy people is that of gross mismanagement of their goods, at the expense of the poor and needy people of the world. They were guilty of hoarding, and wastefulness! Jesus issued several warnings about this sort of thing that has relevance to the passage at hand:

> "Do not store up for yourselves treasures on earth, where moths and vermin destroy, and where thieves break in and steal. [20]But store up for yourselves treasures in heaven, where moths and vermin do not destroy, and where thieves do not break in and steal. (Matthew 6:19-20)

> And he told them this parable: "The ground of a certain rich man yielded an abundant harvest. [17]He thought to himself, 'What shall I do? I have no place to store my crops.' [18]"Then he said, 'This is what I'll do. I will tear down my barns and build bigger ones, and there I will store my

surplus grain. [19]And I'll say to myself, "You have plenty of grain laid up for many years. Take life easy; eat, drink and be merry."' [20]"But God said to him, 'You fool! This very night your life will be demanded from you. Then who will get what you have prepared for yourself?' [21]"This is how it will be with whoever stores up things for themselves but is not rich toward God." (Luke 12:16-21)

Sell your possessions and give to the poor. Provide purses for yourselves that will not wear out, a treasure in heaven that will never fail, where no thief comes near and no moth destroys. [34]For where your treasure is, there your heart will be also. (Luke 12:33-34)

In each of these examples, Jesus speaks against storing up things on the earth and finding security in those possessions. They are all perishable goods that have no eternal value. Believers are to store up their treasures in heaven by committing good deeds for the Lord, which will pay eternal dividends. The fact that people were guilty of hoarding goods to an extreme is an indication of where their hearts were (Luke 12:34).

A courtroom drama now takes place with the prosecuting attorney presenting evidence before the judge. James declares that "their corrosion will testify against you and eat your flesh like fire." Their wastefulness and disregard for the poor testifies to the condition of their hearts, and puts them in a place where they are storing up judgment to come upon them by their selfish extravagant lifestyle. How ironic this courtroom drama is, because the rich were swindling the poor by manipulating the courts for their purposes! James makes it clear to the rich that they will have their day in God's court, where the evidence presented against them will provide clear testimony to their mismanagement and sin of hoarding! God had a concern for poor people, such that he built into the social fabric of Israel a means of providing for the needy, so that there would be no poor among God's people (Deu 15:4). The prophets harshly rebuked the leaders of the nation for their neglect of the poor and disenfranchised (Amos 2:7, 4:1, 5:11-12).

"Their corrosion will testify against you and eat your flesh like fire" is a reference to God's judgment. The prophet Malachi used the imagery of fire when speaking of the day of judgment:

> "Surely the day is coming; it will burn like a furnace. All the arrogant and every evildoer will be stubble, and the day that is coming will set them on fire," says the LORD Almighty. "Not a root or a branch will be left to them." (Malachi 4:1)

The final place where all the wicked throughout world history are retained is referred to as the Lake of Fire (Rev 19:20, 20:14-15). God's judgment is imminent and certain! It doesn't even appear that there is any chance of repentance for the rich.

The sin they are guilty of is "hoarding wealth in the last days." When the day of Pentecost came we entered into a period of salvation history known as the last days or the end times. This era of history will come to its conclusion at the return of the Lord Jesus. In other words, time is running out! The Lord's coming is at hand and could happen at any moment. It appears as though James thought it was forthcoming and might occur within his lifetime.

When the Lord returns it will be a great moment for the people of God, for that is our blessed hope in this life! For those who reject God, like the wealthy James is addressing, it will be a time of unimaginable grief that will be characterized by weeping and wailing! The fact that this age is coming to an end should provide incentive to focus on the things of the Lord, rather than living a hedonistic lifestyle—hoarding goods one couldn't possibly use in a lifetime. People of means should adopt a perspective of life that prohibits them from storing up goods for tomorrow's party, because one day they will stand before God and answer for their actions!

Look! The wages you failed to pay the workers who mowed your fields are crying out against you. The cries of the harvesters have reached the ears of the Lord Almighty. (5:4)

James presents more evidence against them, making their guilt more certain! They withheld wages from their workers. These wealthy landowners were gobbling up land and many people lost their property to these land barons. They had no other option than to work for these landlords, often times as day laborers who received their pay at the end of the day (Mat 20:1-16). In a poor culture where people survived by the skin of their teeth, prompt payment was necessary for their survival. These ultra rich people didn't have the decency to pay their workers—they were ripping them off! James may have had Deuteronomy 24:15 in mind: "Pay him his wages each day before sunset, because he is poor and is counting on it. Otherwise he may cry to the LORD against you, and you will be guilty of sin."

James says the wages are crying out against the guilty parties. Certainly, this is an allusion to Cain's blood crying out to God for justice (Gen 4:10). Those day laborers who cried out to the Lord about the injustices they were suffering, can be assured that God heard their cries. Whenever God's people cry out to the Lord for mercy God will respond, just as he did when his people cried out to him in Egypt. The Lord Almighty is the Lord *Sabaoth*, which is more literally rendered "Lord of hosts", or "Lord of armies". This presents a frightening picture of the Lord leading the armies of heaven against these unrighteous rich people, and gives us further insight into why James instructs them to weep and wail for the misery coming upon them. This is getting worse by the moment for the guilty parties!

You have lived on earth in luxury and self-indulgence. You have fattened yourselves in the day of slaughter. ⁶You have condemned and murdered the innocent one, who was not opposing you. (5:5-6)

They have lived an opulent lifestyle, not denying any of their desires, swindling the poor, and being wasteful to an extreme! They get an F minus in their grade for stewardship! "Self-indulgence" (*spatalao*) certainly has a sinful twist to it. When people are in a position to gratify their desires, barring none, and have the resources to do so, their behavior often plunges into extremes of debauchery. Those who live with no self-control, letting their passions run wild, may find themselves mastered by the things that gave them pleasure. Paul described the widow who lives for self-indulgence (*spatalao*) as being dead even while she lives (1 Tim 5:6). When people use their wealth to gratify their sinful desires while showing no regard for the poor, or God, they are as good as dead! They face the future of certain judgment!

James presents another colorful picture for his readers. Their self-indulgent lifestyle is compared to a domestic animal being fattened for the slaughter. Animals gorge themselves before the slaughter not knowing that they are the main course for dinner! As these rich people gorge their sinful appetites, they are fattening themselves for the impending day of God's judgment, which often times is described as a slaughter. For example, Isa 34:6-8 uses this imagery to describe God's judgment in the land of Edom:

> The sword of the Lord is bathed in blood, it is covered with fat—the blood of lambs and goats,

fat from the kidneys of rams. For the LORD has a
sacrifice in Bozrah and a great slaughter in the
land of Edom. ⁷And the wild oxen will fall with
them, the bull calves and the great bulls. Their
land will be drenched with blood, and the dust
will be soaked with fat. ⁸For the LORD has a day
of vengeance, a year of retribution, to uphold
Zion's cause.

Totally irresponsible with the use of their goods, ignoring
all warnings, insensitive to the needs of the poor they have
swindled, they continue down a path that will take them to
God's slaughterhouse! They will face an eternity separated
from Christ, unless they repent!

It is implied that the rich people were utilizing the courts to
line their pockets with more money. The word condemned is
(*katadikazo*) and carries with it the idea of making a judgment
against or pronouncing guilty. Courts are supposed to render
justice, however, where people have money they have influence.
The poor had no means of defending themselves in the court
system! How can you defeat a "dream team" of highly paid
lawyers when you have a court appointed attorney!

The manner in which they were manipulating the courts isn't
described. Perhaps, they were moving boundary markers (Deu
19:14, 27:17), paying bribes (Deu 10:17-19), not returning things
taken in pledge from the poor (Deu 24:12-13), or perjuring
themselves (Deu 19:16-20). Whatever their methods were, they
were successful in bringing much suffering to people whose
lives were already filled with hardship.

Their last crime is now stated: "you have condemned and
murdered the innocent one, who was not opposing you." How
do we understand murder? Did they have to get rid of some

people to get their way, so they disposed of them? Or was it that their activity led to the poor being thrown in prison because they were unable to pay their debts. Most likely the rich land barons took the indebted small farmers to court, and were able to strip them of their land, then hired them back as sharecroppers, or day laborers. They then found themselves in a position where they worked "dirt cheap", not generating enough income to pay their debts, and could be thrown into debtor's prison where they could spend the rest of their lives.

The conditions in these prisons were deplorable and unless someone bailed you out, you never made it out alive! Indirectly, this is the way in which they were murdering innocent people, but there probably were violent murders taking place as well. Given the description of the guilty parties, it appears as though they have no scruples, using any means whatsoever to get what they want!

The "innocent one" that James refers to is literally "innocent man" or "righteous man" in the original language. Some commentators take this as a reference to Jesus, and some to James. If it refers to James, one would assume this letter was put together by someone after James' martyrdom by pasting his notes together. Both these options are unlikely; therefore, the best way to understand "innocent one" is to take it as a collective singular, describing all the righteous people that suffered at the hands of the rich.

The poor, suffering as they were, didn't oppose the rich. This reflects an attitude that Christians are to display in the face of suffering that Jesus described (Mat 5:39-41). Rather than trying to take up arms and retaliate in kind, James' people followed Jesus' example of non-retaliation described for us in 1 Peter 2:23: "When they hurled their insults at him, he did not retaliate;

when he suffered, he made no threats. Instead, he entrusted himself to him who judges justly."

The world's way of handling injustices is to fight back, retaliate, and get even. However, the Christian is called to patiently trust God in the midst of injustices and always be on his best behavior (1 Peter 4:19). That James' congregation is responding as they did, by walking in Jesus' footsteps, makes the crimes of the rich all the more flagrant!

When this sermon was read aloud one can only imagine how it was received. If some of the rich unbelievers were in attendance, what would they have done after this was read? Get up and leave! Lodge a protest! Turn red in the face with embarrassment, laugh, or get angry? We don't know, but it can be safely concluded that the people who were suffering would take comfort knowing that God was acutely aware of their plight.

When God's people are in dire straits because of injustices being suffered, they often wonder if God knows what's going on, and if he hears their cries. Throughout the ages God's people have asked the question posed by the martyrs under the altar in the book of Revelation (6:10): They called out in a loud voice, "How long, Sovereign Lord, holy and true, until you judge the inhabitants of the earth and avenge our blood?" James' suffering congregation can take comfort in knowing that God sees it all, and is going to do something about it. He will avenge them and make it right!

Insights and Application, (5:1-6)

This passage brings to one's attention the age-old question: "Why does God allow innocent people to suffer gross injustices?" This is a question most people ponder at different points of their lives, especially when they personally go through a painful injustice. We often wonder how it is that the guilty can get away with it! This passage brings to mind the fact that nobody gets away with anything, because everybody stands before God on judgment day and has to answer for their deeds.

For those who are the guilty perpetuators of evil, judgment day will be awful and terrifying. For the oppressed who endure suffering, knowing that God will not leave the guilty unpunished is comforting. God is a righteous judge, who will render perfect justice on that day, so God's people who are being oppressed will be vindicated. God will repay all guilty parties for their evil deeds, and there is comfort for the innocent in knowing that.

One reason that Scripture teaches us not to take matters into our own hands, seeking revenge on those who have wronged us, is that God will take care of it for us! Paul addressed this issue in Romans 12:17-21, citing well-known Old testament texts:

> Do not repay anyone evil for evil. Be careful to do what is right in the eyes of everyone. [18]If it is possible, as far as it depends on you, live at peace with everyone. [19]Do not take revenge, my dear friends, but leave room for God's wrath, for it is written: "It is mine to avenge; I will repay," says the Lord. [20]On the contrary: "If your enemy is hungry, feed him; if he is thirsty, give him something to drink. In doing this, you will heap burning coals on his head." [21]Do not be overcome by evil, but overcome evil with good.

This is a hard truth to live out in everyday experience. When someone wrongs us our sinful tendency is seek revenge and retaliate in kind, except we try to get in the last and best punch.

However, this isn't the Kingdom way. The believer trusts God to take care of it as the righteous judge, who will avenge those who have been wronged. Knowing this brings comfort to God's people! If God didn't hold the evil-doer accountable, what kind of judge would he be! If he let everything slide, and excused the terrible deeds that caused a world of suffering, how could God be considered a righteous judge? He couldn't be! That's the good news; he will avenge his people.

The Christian response to evil-doers is to turn the other cheek. Rather than retaliating, the believer overcomes evil with good. By displaying love to our oppressors Scripture says it is like heaping burning coals on their heads. This is a hard truth to apply to everyday life because our natural tendency isn't to give love to those who hurt us! We want to get even and start swinging.

The prophet Nahum delivered an oracle against Nineveh, the capital of the Assyrian Empire. God's patience with Nineveh had run out and Nahum was sent to prophesy the downfall of the evil empire. He gives us a glimpse into God's sense of justice in Nahum 1:2-3a:

> The Lord is a jealous and avenging God; the Lord takes vengeance and is filled with wrath. The Lord takes vengeance on his foes and vents his wrath against his enemies. ³The LORD is slow to anger but great in power; the Lord will not leave the guilty unpunished.

The Assyrians were ruthless, brutal people. On their campaigns of conquest they inflicted unimaginable suffering everywhere they went. For a great deal of Israel's history, they lived under the constant threat of invasion from the north by the Assyrians. Eventually, the Assyrians invaded the Northern Kingdom and

God's people were deported. A tragic time in the history of Israel, however, God would not leave the guilty Assyrians unpunished for their brutality and crimes against humanity! Nahum prophesied the downfall of Nineveh and ends his oracle with an expression of thankfulness over God's righteous judgment in 3:19:

> Nothing can heal you; your wound is fatal. All who hear the news about you clap their hands at your fall, for who has not felt your endless cruelty?

When Nineveh fell it was a time for all those who felt her sting to rejoice because God—the righteous judge—has avenged all those who suffered under her cruelty. Likewise, oppressed people can rejoice in the knowledge that God will not leave the guilty unpunished in all eras of world history. We all have injustices occur in our lives and it is comforting to know that God is a perfect judge who lets nobody get away with anything.

A second theme to consider from this passage is stewardship. The rich people James addressed were guilty of hoarding more goods than they could ever use, and they rotted away. Recently, a missionary spoke at my church about a time in his life when he had successfully pursued the American Dream and accumulated a lot of stuff: cars, investment properties, TVs, computers, etc. and had more things than he could ever use. As he was feeling the call of God on his life to do missionary work in China, he realized he had to simplify his life and get rid of much of the stuff he had amassed. He sold his property, paid off his cars becoming debt-free, and experienced a moment of liberation. Most of us have closets that are bursting at the seams, have our basements and garages full of things we don't use but others could benefit from. We can't be wasteful with what God has given us.

Chapter Seventeen

"Coping Through Patience"

James 5:7-12

Be patient, then, brothers and sisters, until the Lord's coming. See how the farmer waits for the land to yield its valuable crop, patiently waiting for the autumn and spring rains. [8]You too, be patient and stand firm, because the Lord's coming is near. [9]Don't grumble against one another, brothers and sisters, or you will be judged. The Judge is standing at the door! [10]Brothers and sisters, as an example of patience in the face of suffering, take the prophets who spoke in the name of the Lord. [11]As you know, we count as blessed those who have persevered. You have heard of Job's perseverance and have seen what the Lord finally brought about. The Lord is full of compassion and mercy.

Above all, my brothers and sisters, do not swear—not by heaven or by earth or by anything else. All you need to say is a simple "Yes" or "No." Otherwise you will be condemned.

James has just described in detail the terrifying judgment that was unfolding for the oppressors of his congregations. He described it in the previous section as if it had already started. James has indicated that the rich were guilty of hoarding wealth in the last days, reminding his readers that time is running out! This age ends when the Lord Jesus returns, and all the suffering that God's people have endured will come to a screeching halt.

When will the Lord return? Nobody knows, but the authors of Scripture indicate that it could be at any moment, therefore, the believer should be ready. In the mean time life goes on and all we can do is wait patiently for the Lord to intervene in world history. Believers through the millennia have waited patiently for Christ to return, and bring their hardships to an end. There was little or nothing that the poor people could do to bring the powerful rich to justice, except pray about it and wait. Coping with injustices and living in dire straits requires the virtue of patience. It is to a discussion of this virtue that James brings his readers.

Be patient, then, brothers and sisters, until the Lord's coming. (5:7a)

James commands his readers to be patient, which is the translation of the Greek word *makrothumeo.* The word carries the meaning of being long suffering, bearing up under pressure, and persevering in the midst of insults and injuries from other people while keeping a cool head! Those who possess this virtue have the ability to refrain from lashing out in retaliation against those who have offended them. This virtue is listed as one of the fruit of the Spirit (Gal 5:22) indicating that the Spirit of God produces this virtue in the believer. In other words, patience is the byproduct of genuine faith! In light of the Lord's coming people need to walk in this supernatural patience, knowing that the Lord will avenge them and settle all matters.

The patience that James has described is not accomplished through a passive waiting for the trial to pass. This type of patience calls for an active forbearance of others and a deep trust in the Lord to intervene.

James uses the term "brothers and sisters" for the eleventh time in his homily, reminding them of their familial relationships. The body of Christ waits for the Lord to return *(parousia)*, which refers to the second coming of the Lord and has the basic meaning of presence. The word was used to describe the arrival of a King, and was used by the early Christians to refer to Jesus' coming. Nobody knows when the Lord will return, but the Scripture presents the return of Christ as imminent, which means that it could happen any time. It seems as though James was expecting the Lord to return within his lifetime, so his admonition to be patient for this event to occur makes sense. He goes on to develop the theme of patience as a virtue that is necessary to cope with injustices and hardships in this life.

See how the farmer waits for the land to yield its valuable crop, patiently waiting for the autumn and spring rains. (5:7b)

James provides us with an illustration of patience by directing our attention to the farmer. Once the farmer plants his crops there is nothing he can do but let nature run its course. He can't see the seeds planted in the soil, but he knows there is a process taking place underground. Soon he sees the sprouts breaking through the soil and the hope of any farmer is that there will be adequate rainfall to bring a good harvest. There is nothing the farmer can do to bring the rain or make the plants grow any faster. He must patiently wait for nature to run its course and the land will yield its crops. The rains in Palestine came in the spring and fall, and were critical for good harvests.

You too, be patient and stand firm, because the Lord's coming is near. [9]Don't grumble against one another, brothers and sisters, or you will be judged. The Judge is standing at the door! (5:8-9)

Believers are no different than farmers in the sense that there is nothing they can do to make the Lord return, just as there is nothing the farmer can do to make the crops grow faster, and the rain come quicker. Therefore, they are again commanded to be patient, and stand firm, which is a translation of the Greek word *sterizo*. The word carries with it the idea of "making firm", "strengthening" or "establishing". The root, from which the word is derived, means to "prop up" or "make stable". In light of the imminent return of the Lord, believers need to prop themselves up and stabilize themselves, rather than collapsing under the pressures of life, for they know the Lord will return and avenge them.

The Lord is near (*eggizo*) which has the meaning of at hand, to approach, or draw near. The word suggests that the appearing of the Lord could occur at any moment. Every generation of believers since the time of Christ needs to live under the expectation that Christ could return in their lifetime. This was as true in James' day as it is in ours. We need to stabilize ourselves and be strong in the Lord as we wait for him to come. Paul prayed that God would strengthen (*sterizo*) the Thessalonians' hearts, so that they will be blameless and holy in the presence of our God and Father when our Lord Jesus comes with all his holy ones (3:13). This serves as another indication that patience isn't easily attained and it certainly isn't a passive experience!

In the midst of all the difficulties they were going through, it is easy to understand how someone could lose their temper and let somebody have it! James has dealt extensively with sins of speech, and develops the theme further in this section. Perhaps, some folks were blaming the people around them for the problems they were going through, and were going off on them. It isn't uncommon for people to take it out on others when things aren't going well, so James commands them not to "grumble against each other", especially since they are brothers in the Lord.

They should be supportive of each other rather than taking their frustrations out on their fellow Christians. Grumble is the word *stenazo* and means to sigh or groan inwardly. People get worked up on the inside—becoming bitter—and start taking it out on others by their constant whining and complaining! Their inner life comes out inappropriately!

If they continue to grumble against each other they position themselves to receive God's judgment. James has been describing the fact that judgment has already begun on the rich oppressors, and that the Lord's return is imminent. In light of this, they should be on their best behavior so that when the Lord returns he doesn't have to offer any correction to them. This admonition should bring to mind Jesus' teaching on judging: "Do not judge, or you too will be judged (Matt. 7:1)." The Lord is depicted as standing at the door knocking in Revelation 3:20. When certain signs are fulfilled one can know the appearing *(parousia)* is right at the door (Matt 24:32, Mark 13:29). The door imagery enhances the concept of imminence and the nearness of his coming. James presents his readers with a picture of the Lord standing at the door about to turn the doorknob and come rushing in to begin judgment! This imagery should cause his readers to stop and think, before they give somebody a verbal blast!

Brothers and sisters, as an example of patience in the face of suffering, take the prophets who spoke in the name of the Lord. (5:10)

James provides his readers with an example of patience in the midst of suffering by pointing to the prophets. He doesn't specify which ones, but by reviewing the history of God's prophets a list can easily be compiled of those who suffered as they spoke in the name of the Lord. A story could be written about each prophet and how they endured their struggles, but time and space doesn't permit that in this commentary. Consider Moses, Isaiah, Jeremiah, Ezekiel, Daniel, and others who endured intense suffering and injustices, but were able to endure with God's strength.

The Lord called upon his prophets to deliver a message to the people and they didn't back down! They boldly spoke in the name of the Lord, even though it brought much heat on them. They had the courage to say "Thus says the Lord"! The essence of patience (*makrothumia*)—is to bear up under injustices and wait for the Lord to vindicate their cause, as was demonstrated by the prophets. Anybody who boldly speaks in the name of the Lord—being a truth-teller—will inevitably face a degree of persecution. When God's people speak His word they must do so with gentleness and respect, lest they damage the message (1 Pet 3:15).

As you know, we count as blessed those who have persevered. You have heard of Job's perseverance and have seen what the Lord finally brought about. The Lord is full of compassion and mercy. (5:11)

As we look back on the great men and women of God, and read about them in our daily devotionals we hold them in high esteem! They were able to get the job done for the Lord while enduring the hardships that confronted them, so we consider them blessed! What a privilege to be able to serve the Lord as they did and have his blessing upon them. The words of Jesus come to our attention:

> "Blessed are you when people insult you, persecute you and falsely say all kinds of evil against you because of me. [12]Rejoice and be glad, because great is your reward in heaven, for in the same way they persecuted the prophets who were before you." (Matt 5:11-12)

Jesus' statement brings to mind what James said in 1:12: "Blessed is the one who perseveres under trial because, having stood the test, that person will receive the crown of life that the Lord has promised to those who love him."

The common denominator in the above passages is the rewards given out to the faithful ones who persevere! Whether it is being persecuted for your faith in Christ, or enduring hardships, those who stay the course will be richly rewarded! This should provide incentive to James' readers to hang in there, knowing that there will be a payoff for their efforts!

An example of spiritual stamina is Job! Next to Jesus, Job has been regarded by Christians throughout the ages as the quintessential man of suffering! One associates suffering with the mention of his name. Job's hardships included the loss of his children, his wealth, and his health, which would be enough to make any person susceptible to discouragement, and raise numerous questions about God's intentions. Job didn't have a spotless spiritual performance in the whole matter. He cursed the day of his birth (3:1), appeared a bit self-righteous, he complained, expected an explanation from God about his circumstances, and appeared to be quite impatient (Job 7:11-21; 10:18-22; 13:20-27; 23:2-7; 30:2-23)!

However, through all the suffering Job hung there and never walked away from God. In the midst of the hardships that he experienced the Bible says that Job did not sin against God in anything that he said (1:22; 2:10). His statement, "Though he slay me, yet will I hope in him" (13:15a) is a reflection of his deep faith in God and his spiritual endurance in facing hardships.

James' congregations were facing extreme difficulties and could easily identify with Job! He stands as an example of spiritual stamina for believers of all eras to follow as they face difficult times. The way it ended for Job wasn't all that bad. God rewarded him for his perseverance and restored his wealth, he had more children, and lived to a ripe old age of 140 (Job 42:10-17).

The way the story concludes for Job isn't the way it ends for every believer who goes through extreme suffering! Not all trials end with God richly blessing as he did Job, but blessing or no blessing "the Lord is full of compassion and mercy"! When going through difficult times believers tend to question whether God is compassionate and merciful. The answer is a resounding yes! Job gained profound insights into the Lord's compassion and mercy by going through his trials.

Key to understanding James illustration about the life of Job, is what the Lord finally brought about in his life. In other words, what was the purpose that God had for Job in all the suffering? There were many things that Job didn't understand about everything that occurred, for God didn't answer all of his questions. He was left somewhat in the dark about a great many things. God's purpose in this trial wasn't to provide Job with a detailed list of why everything happened as it did. God's purpose was to bring Job to a deeper level of trust in him, which is the goal God has in mind for all believers that go through difficulties!

Additionally, going through the fire of tribulation has a purifying effect on one's character! James has already discussed with his readers the spiritual benefits that are derived from suffering through trials (1:1-5). As difficult as this was for Job, one can only imagine how Job grew as a believer through this dreadful experience. Perhaps, he developed more compassion for others, became more humble, had greater faith, grew a deeper prayer life, and much more. This is of utmost importance in the grand scheme of eternity, and brings the reminder to our attention that in all things God works for the good of those who love him, who have been called according to his purpose (Ro 8:28).

Prohibition Against Oaths, (5:12)

Above all, my brothers and sisters, do not swear—not by heaven or by earth or by anything else. All you need to say is a simple "Yes" or "No." Otherwise you will be condemned. (5:12)

It is difficult to see a connection with what precedes this verse and what comes after it. It appears to stand on its own, as a random thought, as James winds down to present a last few thoughts to close out his homily. Certainly, James' discussion of oath-taking fits into his larger discussion about sins of the tongue, which has occupied a significant amount of space in his sermon. Taking oaths was a practice that regularly occurred in Jewish culture, and was carried over into the church. Where written contracts were not in use, two people would take an oath with God as witness between them. If one party violated his oath, it was thought that God would judge the offender, thus, not keeping your oath was considered very serious business! It was a matter of integrity before God and man to keep your word.

In Jesus' day oath-taking had degenerated into a deceptive practice. The Jews distinguished between binding and non-binding oaths. Oaths that were taken in the name of God were considered to be binding, but oaths that were taken naming the Temple, the altar, heaven, or anything else were not binding oaths and could be broken without incurring God's judgment. In other words, people would make an oath when in fact they had no intention of keeping their word. They were being deceptive and dishonest. This is the type of sin that both Jesus and James were condemning. Because of the similarities verse 12 has with Matthew 5:33-37, and 23:16-22, one assumes James was familiar with Jesus' teaching on oath-taking.

Above all, my brothers and sisters, do not swear—not by heaven or by earth or by anything else. All you need to say is a simple "Yes" or "No." Otherwise you will be condemned. (5:12)

When James says "above all" it appears that he has something that is of special importance to tell his readers. This verse provides a literary transition to the ending section of his letter, and is the conclusion of a number of things he has said about sins of the tongue. It could be that James considers keeping your word to be one of the greatest markers of personal integrity! Understood this way, all that James has said about personal communication comes to a crescendo in verse 12 with his prohibition on taking oaths.

James again, identifies with his congregation by calling them "brothers and sisters" and continues to speak with a pastor's heart. There is no tone of condemnation in his voice, for he speaks to them as if he is in the audience with them. When James says "do not swear" he isn't referring to using foul language, or taking the Lord's name in vain. He is referring to taking oaths. Oath taking wasn't forbidden in the Old Testament, but it was assumed that the people would keep their word. James may have been drawing from Leviticus 19:12 as he wrote this section: "Do not swear falsely by my name and so profane the name of your God. I am the LORD." Making an oath in the name of the Lord was serious business! If the oath wasn't kept it was thought to be an affront to God's name—bringing his judgment upon the guilty party.

A good argument can be made for the 19th chapter of Leviticus having occupied a central place in James thinking as he wrote this sermon, because he addressed a number of ethical concerns from the same chapter (see introduction). One can see the similarities between Jesus teaching in the Sermon on the Mount and James:

> "Again, you have heard that it was said to the people long ago, 'Do not break your oath, but fulfill to the Lord the vows you have made.' 34But I tell you, do not swear an oath at all: either by heaven, for it is God's throne; 35or by the earth, for it is his footstool; or by Jerusalem, for it is the city of the Great King. 36And do not swear by your head, for you cannot make even one hair white or black. 37All you need to say is simply 'Yes' or 'No'; anything beyond this comes from the evil one. (Matthew 5:33-37)

It was taught that vows made to the Lord were binding and all others could be broken. People made oaths and would swear by the Temple, the altar, by Jerusalem, or the gold in the Temple, and it was thought these oaths were nonbinding. They would enter these oaths with the intent of deceiving the other party. The point that James and Jesus both make, is that when you swear by anything you must keep your word! God calls you to account!

James ends this verse with a warning: Let your "Yes" be yes, and your "No," no, or you will be condemned. The word condemned is the Greek word *krisis,* which is used in the New Testament to describe God's judgment of sinners to eternal separation from God in hell. Perhaps, James' usage of the word is to point out how serious a sin this is. Oath-breaking is a reflection of a deep problem with one's heart. True integrity is found in the man whose word is as good as gold. His "yes" means what he says, and his "no" means what he says. He has no need to take oaths because he keeps his word. His integrity testifies to the genuineness of his faith!

To fit this into the context of James' letter, the one who is transformed by the word of God, and is a doer of the word, has a vibrant faith that manifests in good works, has control over his communication, walks in the wisdom from above, is not having an affair with the world, and walks in humility and repentance will have no need of taking oaths. His word is sufficient, and thus, he proves the veracity of his faith! Those who continue to walk a path of dishonesty, and deception, through false oath-taking, are displaying characteristics that are inconsistent with those who are true disciple's of Christ!

Insights and Application, (5:7-12)

This passage raises a number of questions that don't have any good answers. Why do Christian's suffer indignities at the hands of rich and powerful nonbelievers? Why do bad things happen to good people? Why does an all-powerful God allow tragedies to occur in the lives of believers? Theologians and philosophers have pondered these questions for millennia, and still do. Everybody who has suffered hardship, or an injustice of some sort has asked these kinds of questions. There are many Christians today that find themselves in similar situations to James' people, where they are being oppressed by their government, persecuted by hostile antagonists, even to the point of being put to death just because they're Christians!

The answer James provides is to wait patiently for the Lord to return and set things straight. This isn't the answer that most people want to hear. In fact, as James homily is being read to his congregation I can just see the disappointed looks on their faces, when he says be patient and wait for the Lord to show up! Naturally, they would rather have God intervene instantly, bring the guilty parties to justice and relieve them of their suffering. Unfortunately, that isn't how God works! He calls for believers to be patient, pray diligently, with the understanding that on judgment day he will settle all accounts and justice will be served!

Being patient in the midst of extreme hardship requires supernatural strength, which God provides through His Spirit. In our human sinfulness when we are wronged the natural response is to strike back and smash your opponent—revenge is sweet! But that's not God's way. He calls us to keep a cool head, with the understanding that he is working things out on a daily basis, in ways that we may have little or no understanding about. This is the challenge of living by faith; moment-by-moment trusting the Lord is working all things together for the good of those who love him (Ro 8:28), even if we don't see how! Patience is a byproduct of faith in Christ!

When people are under duress things can get out of control! Tempers flare, people blame their circumstances on others, and things can get outright ugly! Such was the case for James' readers. Under the pressure and hardship they were enduring, I'll bet it wasn't uncommon for people to blow a gasket and go off on someone! This is where patience comes into the picture again. Under stress patience has to govern one's behavior, such that people aren't complaining, whining, and backbiting each other!

Years ago I knew of two Christian guys that worked for an insurance company that was restructuring their organization, which meant lots of people got pink slips and were looking for a job! The amount of work remained the same, so everybody's workload increased and the pay remained the same. Those who survived the cuts were putting in long hours, and they didn't like it! Tempers were short, conflict scenarios emerged, there was complaining, some workers got fed up and quit—it wasn't a pretty picture!

The two Christian employees were in middle management, and were working closely with a man (a nonbeliever) who was high up in the company. After many months of the work environment being a high stress zone, the two Christians were sitting down drinking coffee in the break room after a long day, and the head guy came in taking a seat at the table. He told them how difficult this time had been for him personally because of the constant complaining of the people, and the conflict that he constantly had to deal with. He expressed his appreciation to each of them for a job well done, and said of all the people working in this office the two of you are the only ones who didn't have a meltdown, blow a fuse, or loose it! What's with you guys?

They told him they're Christians and they respect their superiors and believe in doing their work as if it is for the Lord. They went on to share the gospel and tell him more about their faith and the Christian life. What this corporate guru saw in these two Christians, was God's patience at work on a daily basis. It clearly set them apart from the rest of the work force such that he saw something different and admirable in them— supernatural patience!

There is a long and prolific list of prophets that suffered hardship as they spoke the truth for God. Their ability to endure the abuse and persecution directed their way was supernatural! Reading Hebrews chapter 11 will give you an insight into the prophets' ability to draw supernatural strength as they spoke the truth for God.

When I read about Job I can't fathom the anguish he went through! I ask the Lord not to test me as he did Job—I don't need that! God will test our faith at times and in ways that might seem unfair and painful. Job endured his trial without loosing his faith and walking away from the Lord! He never had an answer as to why this trial came into his life. This is the test of faith! Why did God choose Job for this test? Job never got an answer from God as to why this happened. When unfavorable circumstances appear in our life, the test of faith is to keep trusting God and believe that he is good, merciful, and compassionate.

I remember a thought provoking story a missionary told my congregation about what happened to her father when she was a little girl. They were missionaries somewhere in the jungle, and under the cover of darkness some locals kidnapped her father and they never saw him again. Nobody knows what happened to him, but he must have been killed. Her mother said to the children, you can keep trusting God. God is good you can trust him. That was the message she wanted to instill in her little children. Rather than letting this experience poison their hearts against God, she wanted them to move toward God in deeper trust.

That is the essence of a test of faith: you can keep trusting God even when bad things happen to you. When Job lost his children, his wealth, and his health, he could have thrown in the towel and walked away from God, however he didn't. He could have concluded that God has evil intentions for him and isn't to be trusted, but he didn't go there. He kept trusting the Lord, even though he never had the "why did this happen to me" question answered. He serves as an example of persevering faith for all believers to emulate.

Having pastored near Fort Drum in upstate New York, periodically one of our soldiers from the 10th Mountain division would tragically get killed in battle. When you talk to the young wife with little children, and she says, "Why did this happen", there isn't a sufficient answer to give her. Only God can answer that question. We don't have his perspective, but God is good and is worthy of our trust! It is in those moments of anguish that we experience the depth of God's comfort and compassion. These are hard truths for believers to grasp!

It is difficult to see how verse 12 fits into this passage about patience, suffering, and endurance. Often times when people are going through hard times they tend to bargain with God, which is something we've all done. For instance, when struggling we say something like: God if you take this pain away I promise I'll tithe for the rest of my life! In fact, I'll give 15%. I'll never drink again if you will give me what I'm praying for. I'll be in church every week if you deliver me from this situation. Making promises like this demonstrates a lack of faith in God and is a form of oath-taking. It is a form of trying to manipulate God by making promises to him, most of which end up being broken.

Chapter Eighteen

"The Prayer of Faith"

James 5:13-15

Is anyone among you in trouble? Let them pray. Is anyone happy? Let them sing songs of praise. [14]Is anyone among you sick? Let them call the elders of the church to pray over them and anoint them with oil in the name of the Lord. [15]And the prayer offered in faith will make the sick person well; the Lord will raise them up. If they have sinned, they will be forgiven.

It is difficult to find a connection with this section and verse that precedes it. One possible link with verse 12 is that James wants his congregants to pray, rather than making oaths carelessly. The one who makes false oaths is reflecting his lack of faith in God, whereas the one who prays is reflecting his true faith in the Lord. Prayer is the proper response to God when facing difficulties of the magnitude James' people were facing. It appears that James' sermon comes full circle. He began by addressing people in peril with an encouraging word to pray (1:5) now he ends his homily with another word of encouragement to pray.

Some of the people James was ministering to were no doubt struggling spiritually, because of the oppression and suffering they were experiencing. There were those who were spiritually at the end of their rope, while there were people who were suffering physical ailments. James provides instruction about how to pray for people in those circumstances. This passage has been commonly referred to as the "prayer of faith" (v. 15). This is one of the most difficult passages to understand in his homily, and it raises more questions than it answers. However, the meaning is not completely obscured to the reader.

Is anyone among you in trouble? Let them pray. (5:13a)

James is providing instructions to his readers about how they should respond in a variety of circumstances, the first of which is when trouble enters a person's life. "Trouble" is the translation of the word *kakopatheo,* which refers to a variety of sufferings and afflictions. It is the same word he used to describe the suffering of the prophets in verse 10. That James congregations were suffering is obvious from reading through his sermon. The appropriate response is to pray. He doesn't mention what the content of the prayer should be, however, one can infer from the context that the prayer should be for patient endurance, of the kind displayed by Job and the prophets (5:10-11).

Is anyone happy? Let them sing songs of praise. (5:13b)

The second question James presents is addressed to those who are happy, which refers to the inward joyful disposition of the believer. Being in a time of trouble and experiencing happiness appear to be polar opposites! In both extremes the believer can keep the lines of communication open to God through prayer and praise.

The joy we have in Christ is not dependent upon favorable circumstances in life. Even when things are not going well and the believer finds himself in troublesome times, he still has the joy of the Lord in his heart. In fact, James has told his readers that they should consider their trials a source of joy (1:2). This is one of the great things about the Christian life—joy isn't dependent upon favorable circumstances, it is rooted in our relationship with Christ.

When feeling those moments of joy the appropriate response is to sing songs of praise (*psallo*), from which we derive the English word psalms. There is a close connection between prayer and praise, in fact, praise can be considered a form of prayer (Phil 4:6; Col 4:2). A dialogue of prayer and praise should be a constant in a Christian's life. James writes this as an imperative in the present tense, which means this is a command to sing songs of praise on a continual basis.

Is anyone among you sick? Let them call the elders of the church to pray over them and anoint them with oil in the name of the Lord. (5:14)

The third question James asks is addressed to those who are sick (*astheneo*). The Greek word denotes sickness, whether it be physical ailments, spiritual, or mental weakness. Jesus is said to sympathize with our weaknesses (*astheneia*) in Hebrews 4:15, which refers to the comprehensive effects of the fall on the human condition. John 5:3 describes disabled (*astheneo*) people as the blind, the lame, and the paralyzed, thus providing us with a sample of ailments covered by the term.

How severe is the sickness James is describing? It would appear that the illness is very serious since he is instructed to call for the elders to anoint him and pray over him. It would seem that he is bed-ridden since the elders pray over him, and the terms "make the sick person well" and "the Lord will raise him up" all indicate a rather serious malady!

The sick person is instructed to call the elders of the church for prayer. But why call the elders? Why not just have some of your Christian friends pray for you? The elders are in spiritual authority and oversight over the church (Acts 20:28, 1 Pet 5:1-3). Their position implies that they are spiritually mature men who are of good character. When people are seriously ill, it is not uncommon for them to be totally discouraged in their walk with the Lord. Maybe they are at the "end of their rope", and in addition to the elder's prayers for healing, they need some encouragement in the Lord. It is not uncommon for people who are physically sick to be so discouraged that they are having a crisis of faith! That's when the elders step into the picture, and provide spiritual counseling to help the sick person be strengthened in their relationship with God.

The elders are to pray over him, which implies that the person is bed-ridden, and possibly they would lay hands on the sick person as they prayed (Mat 19:13), although this is not mentioned in the instructions.

The elders are to anoint him with oil in the name of the Lord. What is the purpose of the oil? Little is said in Scripture about anointing with oil and its relationship to prayer. Mark 6:13 informs us that the twelve drove out many demons and anointed many sick people with oil and healed them. Anointing with oil was done as part of the burial process, kings were anointed with oil, and the practice served ritual purposes as well. James is the only other author of Scripture, besides Mark, that mentions the practice of anointing with oil in relation to healing. There are three possibilities regarding the function of anointing with oil.

One possibility is that the oil was for medicinal purposes. The anointing (*aleipho*) would be like rubbing oil on the person. Oil had a broad range of medicinal purposes in the ancient world and was probably the most common medication of the day. The elders would therefore be combining the application of medicine with the spiritual activity of praying for healing. In other words, they were functioning as pastors and doctors simultaneously. The weakness of this view is why the elders should be summoned to anoint the sick person with oil if the purpose of this is exclusively medicinal. Surely, someone else beside the elders could do that for the sick person.

The second possibility is the sacramental interpretation, which arose in the early church in a practice called the *euchelaion* (oil for prayer). This led to the practice of extreme unction in the Roman church, which originated in AD 852, and was for the purpose of removing the presence of sin to prepare the dying person to meet his Maker. Since Vatican II the rite has been called "the anointing of the sick." This has virtually no basis in James, for there is no mention of preparation for death in the text under consideration. The weakness of this view is that the anointing isn't what activates God's grace and brings healing! It is the prayer offered in faith that makes the sick person well (v. 15).

The third possibility, and the most commonly accepted today, is that the oil is symbolic of being set apart into God's presence for his caring touch. Kings were anointed with oil as an indication that the Spirit of the Lord was upon them enabling the men to perform their God-given assignment. For example, 1 Samuel 16:13 records the incident of David being anointed King of Israel by the prophet Samuel: "So Samuel took the horn of oil and anointed him in the presence of his brothers, and from that day on the Spirit of the LORD came upon David in power..." The anointing of oil is linked to the presence of the Holy Spirit coming upon David to empower him to complete his duties. The significance of the oil may carry the same link to the Holy Spirit in James as well. This seems to be the most likely meaning of anointing with oil.

The anointing is to be done in the name of the Lord! This brings the Lord into the situation, and he is involved in the entire process of ministering to the sick individual. The "name" is synonymous with one's character, therefore anointing in the name of the Lord is invoking God in all his love, goodness, purity, kindness, mercy, compassion, and so on, to touch the life of the distressed believer. There are no magical properties in the oil, and there is nothing magical in reciting the Lord's name.

And the prayer offered in faith will make the sick person well; the Lord will raise them up. If they have sinned, they will be forgiven. (5:15)

James emphasis in this passage is on prayer offered in faith— not anointing with oil in the name of the Lord. Grammatically, anointing is subordinate to praying with faith in the Lord's name. One might be tempted to think that elders are summoned because they possess the gift of healing (1 Cor 12:9). However, that is not even mentioned in this passage, nor is the gift of healing a prerequisite for eldership. The elder must be a mature Christian who is a man of faith and prayer.

The elders offer a prayer in genuine faith, as they invoke the Lord to bring healing into the sick person's life. James has provided his readers instruction on how to pray in faith, without doubting (1:5-8). This is the kind of faith elders need to generate as they pray over the sick person, and their faith should be typical of that which any mature believer in Christ possesses! Nothing is said about the faith of the sick person. Perhaps, the exercise of his faith is displayed in calling for the elders of the church for prayer on his behalf.

James says the prayer offered in faith will make the sick person well. He introduces the word *kamno*, translated sick, which is different than *astheneo* used in verse 14, also translated sick. Is there any difference in meaning between the two words? *Kamno* covers a variety of symptoms including fatigue, exhaustion (Heb 12:3), even death (Wis 4:16; 15:9). The use of the word *kamno* therefore, sheds more light on the person's condition: in addition to being physically sick the person is utterly exhausted, emotionally drained, spiritually depleted, and totally discouraged. This should come as no surprise, because people who are battling a serious illness may also be very discouraged in their walk with the Lord, and worn down emotionally and spiritually. For example, in Job's agony he said "I loathe my very life; therefore I will give free rein to my complaint and speak out in the bitterness of my soul." (Job 10:1).

The prayer offered in faith will make the sick person "well", is a translation of the Greek word *sozo,* which has a wide range of meanings. It is typically translated "save", but also refers to physical healing in the gospel accounts (Matt. 9:21-22, Mark 3:4, 5:23, 28, 34, 6:56, 10:52, Luke 7:50, 8:48, 50, 17:19, 18:42, & John 11:12). In addition to making the "sick person well, the Lord will raise him up", which means he will be able to stand vertically and get out of bed.

Reading this verse begs for an answer to the question: "why don't we see everyone the elders pray for get healed?" If healing doesn't occur does this imply the elder's faith was deficient? Perhaps, the elders have some sin in their lives such that God didn't honor their prayers! This is unlikely, and there is nothing in the context that would justify such a conclusion.

When it comes to prayer there are two sides to the equation: the first involves our part in making the request in faith, the second part is God's answer! We have no control over how God is going to answer a prayer for healing, or for that matter any other prayer! God is totally sovereign over how he chooses to answer a prayer for healing. Why God chooses to heal some and not others is a divine mystery, and no man has the code to cracking this mystery. The answer to that lies strictly in the mind of God and is beyond our understanding.

The prayer is said to "make the sick person well" (future tense), and the "Lord will raise them up" (future tense). Ultimately speaking, all believers will be healed at the resurrection, but that is not the point James is trying to make in this passage. He is emphasizing God's answer to prayer offered by the elders.

The last thing James says is "if he has sinned, he will be forgiven." This implies that the elders have conducted an interview with the sick person to ascertain the status of his walk with the Lord. They are taking his spiritual temperature to see if there is anything in his life that would require confession and repentance. The elders are to be concerned about the physical health of the person, but at the same time take a look at the quality of the person's spiritual demeanor as well. One might consider this a spiritual diagnostic to determine why the person is suffering. It could be that there is a sin in the person's life to which his illness can be attributed.

In the Old Testament, covenant faithfulness translated into God's blessing of fertility, abundant harvests, victory over enemies, and long life (Deu 28; Lev 26). On the other hand, crop failures, draught, infertility, diseases, and plagues were the result of a breach of covenant faithfulness. No doubt the entire nation, down to each person was aware of the link between sin and physical sickness. Perhaps, this is the background that James has in mind as he writes this verse.

Ultimately speaking, all sickness can be related to sin, because before sin entered the world there was no sickness! The Scriptures do establish a relationship between sin and sickness. For example, the Corinthian believers were guilty of abusing the integrity of the Lord's Supper—they were making a mockery of the body and blood of the Lord! The apostle Paul said: "That is why many among you are weak and sick, and a number of you have fallen asleep. (1 Cor 11:30)." King David goes into great detail about his physical sickness and relates it to his unconfessed sin (Ps 38)! The fact is God does sometimes use physical illnesses to discipline his children for corrective purposes.

Paul had his thorn in the flesh and prayed three times that the Lord would remove it, but he gave Paul a no answer (2 Cor 12:9-10). There were purposes that God was working out in Paul's life through the thorn in the flesh, which actually benefited Paul! God saw it as a form of grace that was for Paul's good, in the sense that it made Paul more humble and useful in serving the Lord. Paul says the thorn in the flesh was given him not as a chastening for sin, but, on the contrary, because of the great revelations he was privileged to receive he might become too bigheaded and prideful. The thorn was God's way of keeping Paul humble, so that he wouldn't let it go to his head and impair his ability to serve.

Finally, there is nothing in James' text that indicates this practice was only for the apostolic age. It appears that this should be a normative practice in the church today.

Insights and Application, (5:13-15)

It should not surprise us that James brings up the theme of prayer again in his homily (1:5-8, 4:2), because he was a man of prayer. He was given the nickname "Camel Knees" because he spent so much time on his knees in prayer that he developed callouses that looked like the knees of a camel. In the previous section James taught that genuine faith produces patience in the life of a believer. In this section James identifies another benchmark of authentic faith, which is excelling in prayer!

James has written a passage of Scripture that gives contemporary Christians a headache in trying to figure out exactly what he means, for there are a variety of ways this passage is understood. Make no mistake about it healing is a very controversial topic in the body of Christ! Numerous church splits have occurred over this issue, entire denominations have split over the issue of healing, and many rifts between believers have occurred over the topic of healing.

There are some believers who claim that it is the right of every child of God to walk in perfect health, if you can believe God for it. Then, there are those Christians who believe that God doesn't heal as he did in the First Century age of the apostles, and there are moderating views between the two extremes.

Those who claim that God guarantees healing to the suffering saint this side of heaven, if the faith to believe for healing can be marshaled, do a great disservice to those who don't experience healing. The sick person is left wallowing in the mud of guilt, because he is he told that he didn't have enough faith to believe God for healing. Perhaps, God didn't heal him because he had unconfessed sin in his life that needed to be dealt with.

Either way, the sick person must battle thoughts of being a second class Christian, while listening to the condemning statements of their fellow believers tell them they lack faith, or need to deal with their unconfessed sin. The error made by those who take this position is thinking they can command God to do what they want to be done! God heals some, but not others, for reasons that are totally unknown to us.

In every church that I've pastored there is always somebody that appears who takes the position that God will heal you, if you can generate the faith to believe it and receive it. Often times they take this position because they had an experience where God healed them! One woman, whom I'll call Terri, claimed she had a miraculous intervention by God, when he totally healed her of a serious malady. Praise the Lord! I have no doubt that God brought physical healing into her life, just as God has brought healing into the lives of many other believers.

Terri's error was in thinking that her experience should be normative for everybody else who is sick in the body of Christ. In other words, she asked God to heal her and he did! Therefore, if you're sick you should ask God to heal you and he will! If he doesn't, there is something deficient in you—lack of faith or unconfessed sin that blocks God's healing power in your life.

She would often approach sick believers with her mantra of God can heal if you can only believe for it. Without realizing it she was actually an agent of condemnation, not encouragement. When people didn't get healed, she would tell them they need to trust more, pray harder, do a spiritual inventory, confess more sin, and then God will intervene; after all, healing is the right of every child of God! You've got to discover what's blocking God's healing power in you.

The elders of the church had to sit down with her and offer a word of correction to her, because she was upsetting the faith of some and propagating error. She ended up leaving the church offering words of condemnation to the church leadership to the effect that they didn't have faith to believe God for his promises. Sadly, she will do the same thing in her next church and will probably end up having a similar result, unless the church leadership takes the same position she does on healing.

We often hear preachers on TV say you're out of God's will if you're sick, but who can be presumptuous in knowing how God is working in the life of a sick person. God may be using an illness for disciplinary purposes to increase faith and dependence on him, to improve one's prayer life, refine character, develop patience, and more. Who can presume to know what God is trying to accomplish in the sick person's life? Nobody can know the mind of God is this!

James said the prayer offered in faith will make the sick person well (v. 15). Praying with faith, like praying in Jesus' name, requires certainty and confidence that God is able to answer that prayer. He has already informed his readers that those who don't possess single-minded faith shouldn't expect to receive anything from the Lord (1:6-8). However, praying with faith also acknowledges God's will, and his sovereignty in all matters of life. When offering up a prayer in faith for one's healing, it must be understood that in some cases it isn't God's will to heal. His will involves purposes other than healing!

Over the years I've done the prayer of faith many times with elders, according to James' instructions. After many years of doing this practice my conclusion is this: sometimes God heals and sometimes he doesn't—there lies the sovereignty of God!

CHAPTER NINETEEN

"PRAYING FOR ONE ANOTHER"

James 5:16-18

Therefore confess your sins to each other and pray for each other so that you may be healed. The prayer of a righteous person is powerful and effective. [17]Elijah was a human being, even as we are. He prayed earnestly that it would not rain, and it did not rain on the land for three and a half years. [18]Again he prayed, and the heavens gave rain, and the earth produced its crops.

This is a passage of Scripture that one hardly sees lived out in the contemporary church. Prayer isn't just for the elders of the church, everybody should be praying for one another. Confessing sins and praying for healing should be a normative practice for God's people, which would yield great spiritual dividends. It is to a discussion of this that we direct our attention.

Prayer Among God's People, (5:16)

Therefore confess your sins to each other and pray for each other so that you may be healed. The prayer of a righteous man is powerful and effective. (5:16)

Prayer for healing is not to be restricted to the elders of the church—it should be a community practice! Confessing sins to each other requires a transparency among God's people that far exceeds what exists in the typical church in America. In the Old Testament, confession of sins was a common practice (Lev 5:5-6; 16:21; 26:40; Ezra 10). On the Day of Atonement the priest would lay his hands on the Scapegoat and confess all the sins of the nation before it was led out into the wilderness (Lev 16:21). Proverbs 28:13 could have been a passage that informed James' understanding as he penned this verse: "He who conceals his sins does not prosper, but whoever confesses and renounces them finds mercy."

James issues this call to confession and prayer in the form of a command, and since it is written in the present tense it is an activity that should be continuously happening! Confessing (*homologeo*) your sins literally means to say the same thing God says, or to agree with God. Thus, the one who confesses his sin is agreeing with God that his behavior is in violation of God's righteous standards, and forgiveness is required. It is implied that the guilty party is also confessing his sins to God, not just the person hearing his confession. One would think that where there is confession there would be forgiveness, but James says healing will result. He is still talking about physical healing, for the Greek word *iaomai* refers to the healing of physical maladies in a number of places (Matt 8:8, 13; 15:28; Mark 5:29; Luke 5:17, 6:18, 19; 7:7). It is implied in the context that God will forgive the sin when it is confessed, so that forgiveness and healing are virtually synonymous in this text.

The passage doesn't specify the circumstances under which the confessing and praying are taking place. Is the one confessing his sins doing so to a brother that he has offended, and therefore is seeking reconciliation with him? The passage doesn't say. Could it be that the one confessing his sin is doing so to a brother because he needs encouragement and prayer support? The text is silent about this matter. The context seems to indicate that confessing isn't limited to people who are in conflict with each other. Certainly, if two Christians are at odds with each other they should confess their sins to each other and pray for reconciliation. It appears that the confessing James has in mind is hurting people who are possibly sick, and need a listening ear, encouragement, and prayer from a fellow Christian.

Bringing sins into the light of God's presence, and other believer's has healing properties. This verse implies that believers need to be equipped to hear someone's confession and pray for them. The entire body of Christ is called into this ministry—there are to be no passive bystanders! The result of this practice is that it brings healing into the life of the sick person, and ensures the health of the church! One can't help seeing a preventative aspect to this practice as well. Regular confession is good for the soul and keeps the body healthy!

The power of prayer is never to be underestimated for James. He has a high regard for prayer throughout his sermon and views prayer as effectual: "The prayer of a righteous man is powerful and effective." The righteous man isn't the "super saint"—it is any Christian! In one sense, all believers in Christ are righteousness because at the moment of their conversion Christ's righteousness is imputed to them. However, it seems that James has something more in mind than this. In the larger context of James' sermon, the one who keeps the ethical demands he has outlined, is the one who is living righteously before God. In the immediate context of his sermon, the one who confesses his sins, and prays for his fellow brothers in Christ is demonstrating the qualities of a righteous life before God.

The one living righteously has great potential in prayer—because it is powerful and effective. "Powerful" translates the Greek word *energeo,* which literally means to work, or to energize. It is a present participle so the idea presented is that the righteous person's prayers are in a perpetual state of energizing, and working. "Effective" *(polyischuo)* translates two Greek words *poly* (much) and *ischyo* (have power, be able to prevail, be strong). By utilizing these two words James is trying to "wow" the reader into understanding how much raw spiritual power is unleashed in prayer! It goes beyond what we are capable of grasping (Eph 3:20).

Every Christian can be powerful and effective in prayer, having the ability to petition God for healing on behalf of their brothers in Christ. This isn't some special gift God gives to a select few, he makes the power of prayer available to all who seek his face and live righteously! This should provide incentive for God's people to raise the bar on their righteous living, and login some time praying.

Elijah: An Example of Powerful and Effective Praying, (5:17-18)

Elijah was a human being, even as we are. He prayed earnestly that it would not rain, and it did not rain on the land for three and a half years. ¹⁸Again he prayed, and the heavens gave rain, and the earth produced its crops.

James likes to provide examples to his readers to drive home his points. He brings Elijah into the picture, who was highly regarded by the Jews as a great prophet and man of prayer. He is known primarily for his spiritual battle with Ahab and Jezebel and the long drought recorded in 1 Kings 17-18. His prayers accomplished amazing results!

Elijah has an impressive resume, which might make following his example seem like an attempt in futility to the average Christian. However, James points out that "Elijah was a man just like us"! There were times when he was discouraged, depressed, suicidal, fearful, and exhausted. He's gone through many of the same "ups and downs" in life as we have, yet he was effective in prayer! This should serve as an incentive for us to pray, for the modern-day believer can identify with Elijah's weaknesses. Rather than regarding Elijah as a "super star" Christian, James would rather have us view him as a sinner just like we are! If Elijah can be dynamic in prayer than we can as well!

The reference to the draught is found in 1 Kings 17-18, with no mention of the precise duration of the draught, nor a reference to Elijah's prayers, with the exception of 1 Kings 18:42. The three and a half year duration of the draught is stated by James and Jesus (Luke 4:25). It is James who attributes the beginning and end of the draught to Elijah's prayers.

In the middle of the draught narrative Elijah is staying at the widow of Zarephath's home and her son died. Elijah swung into action:

> "Then he stretched himself out on the boy three times and cried out to the LORD, "LORD my God, let this boy's life return to him!" 22The LORD heard Elijah's cry, and the boy's life returned to him, and he lived." (1 Kings 17:21-22)

The Jews came to view Elijah as a great man of prayer, which was no doubt influenced by the healing of the widow's son.

Elijah "prayed earnestly" which can more literally be translated "he prayed in prayer." James uses this construction in Greek to highlight the intensity of Elijah's prayers. The beginning and end of the draught are attributed to Elijah's prayers, thus enabling the earth to produce crops.

To reiterate, Elijah's accolades in prayer seem so far beyond the average believer that one would question why James selected him as the example to be followed in prayer. After all, who can control the weather through prayer!

Perhaps, James is challenging his readers to stretch their faith and open new horizons regarding the power of prayer. The Christian life requires vibrant faith, which is best expressed in humble dependence upon God through prayer. The elders of the church who were praying for healing of the sick (vv. 14-15), and those who were praying for the healing of others in the body (v. 16) need to deepen their faith and believe that the impossible comes into the realm of the possible through prayer.

Insights and Application, (5:16-18)

This passage has body ministry written all over it! Praying for one another isn't just for elders, the senior pastor, small group leaders, etc., it should be a practice all Christians are committed too. Sadly, it has virtually disappeared in the modern church. John and Charles Wesley had great success applying the practice of praying for one another in developing the Methodist brand of Christian faith, in eighteenth Century England.

This passage does raise a number of questions that must be thought through. Does the one confessing ask the listener to forgive him? Does the one hearing the confession say I forgive you? Are specific sins to be named by the one confessing? Is James thinking about two believers who are at odds with each other, confessing and praying for one another to resolve conflict and restore their relationship? If you sin against God is it right to ask forgiveness from your brothers?

These questions are not answered in the text, but the words of Jesus recorded in John 20:23 help shed some light on this issue: "If you forgive anyone's sins, their sins are forgiven; if you do not forgive them, they are not forgiven."

The context of the James' passage indicates the result of the confessing and praying is healing (of all types). Certainly, this would include two believers who are at odds with each other and need to confess their sins to one another and pray for each other. The result of said activity is a cleansing of the soul. The poison of bitterness, or anger that is burning in your soul, and guilt you carry because of something you did or said can all be cleared away through mutual confession and prayer. Believers at odds with each other should seek forgiveness, however the practice James is advocating is much broader than that. James is presenting his readers with a general practice (confession and prayer) that has very broad application. This practice can be applied one-on-one, in a small group setting with several people, or even in a larger group of people.

Having a trusted friend that you can be transparent with and share your struggles with is therapeutic. For many years I met with a close friend every week and we would talk about life! Our level of trust was deep enough such that we could share anything with each other free of condemnation. We would tell each other the areas that we messed up during the week, the result of which was always mutual encouragement, and cleansing of the soul. We were both honest enough with each other that we had no problem calling each to the carpet when needed. We didn't stroke each other and make excuses for our behavior, we related to one another in brutal honesty, yet with love! Being able to offload guilt, stress, and anxiety through spiritual conversations does have a healing effect. There are times when one can be so overwhelmed with sins, that you need to confess your struggles to someone and get the burdens off your chest. Having a trusted brother to pray for you can strengthen your resolve to press on in the Christian life.

There are other ways that this principle of confession and prayer can be put to practice. Recently, a friend of mine who attends a mega church told me about an associate pastor who stood before the congregation and made a confession. After his wife passed away he had entered into a relationship with a married women that was inappropriate. He confessed his sin to the elders of the church, and during a Sunday service confessed his sin to the entire congregation, asking for their forgiveness. At the conclusion of the service many people embraced him, extended forgiveness to him, and offered to keep him in their prayers. No doubt, there was a healing effect for the pastor.

Another example of the restorative value of confession and prayer occurred during one of the weekly worship team practices, in a church I was pastoring. One of the musicians lost it and went off on the leader, yelled at him and then walked out. Everybody in attendance was stunned and needless to say the practice went downhill from there. During the week I talked to the person and called him on his behavior, telling him he should confess his sin to the group and apologize for his outburst. He acknowledged his guilt and agreed to do so. At the next practice with all in attendance he apologized to the worship leader for yelling at him, and then apologized to everybody else for his angry outburst, seeking forgiveness from all. There was a time of prayer and the effect of that was healing for the entire team. Restoration occurred and the worship team once again had unity.

No doubt, there are many other examples of James' principle that could be cited here, but these examples should serve to illustrate his point. Anytime confession and prayer are combined there is a healing effect in the body of Christ. I hope every Christian has a person in her life that she can be open and transparent with. The problem is that Christians today are too embarrassed to confess their sins, and are afraid of being shamed if they lay their cards on the table!

In vv. 17-18, James directs his readers to the example of Elijah as a great man of prayer. James thinks we can pray like Elijah! You've got to be kidding! That seems to be the typical response when this passage is read. After all, there were amazing answers to prayer that were affected through Elijah, but we get a glimpse into his humanity—which is what James is emphasizing here.

In so many ways Elijah was just like us. He is a sinner who goes through the same things you and I go through: depression, anxiety, suicidal tendencies, exhaustion, fearful moments, bad decisions, lack of trusting God, and so forth. At times, modern-day Christians set the Biblical characters on such a pedestal that we forget that they are people no different than we are. All the Biblical characters had their flaws, bad habits, and quirks, yet that's just the point—God still used them in amazing ways to accomplish his purposes.

James firmly believes prayer is powerful and effective, thus we should view prayer in the same way. This passage is designed to stretch your faith and stimulate you to pray more, with a new sense of expectation of what God can do through the prayers of his people. It is thought provoking to consider the fruit that could emerge from a church that instills the practice of confession and prayer into its existence. The results could be as monumental as the prayers of Elijah!

Chapter Twenty

"Reclaiming a Brother"

James 5:19-20

My brothers and sisters, if one of you should wander from the truth and someone should bring that person back, ²⁰remember this: Whoever turns a sinner from the error of their way will save them from death and cover over a multitude of sins.

This brings us to the grand finale of James' sermon. James has been stressing the importance of confessing sins to one another, and praying for one another as a community practice. Each believer must have a vested interest in the welfare of his fellow worshipers. When someone in the body of Christ backslides, or becomes a dropout, how can the faithful members of a church help him? There should be a concerted effort by God's people to reclaim the brother. Certainly prayer, which is powerful and effective, can be utilized as a way to bring the person back to the place he should be spiritually. James brings us to a discussion of how believers can reclaim a brother who is in grave spiritual danger.

My brothers and sisters, if one of you should wander from the truth and someone should bring that person back, [20]remember this: Whoever turns a sinner from the error of their way will save them from death and cover over a multitude of sins. (5:19-20)

The person who wanders from the truth is clearly a believer since James begins his address with "my brothers and sisters", which is a term for fellow believers that James has used repeatedly throughout his homily. "If one of you" clearly refers to the brothers and sisters—the community of believers in Christ. There is nothing in the passage that would indicate that the wanderer is a professing believer only, who hasn't been regenerated, or a nominal Christian, or a backslider, or a seeker who lost interest. Most likely, such categories didn't even exist in the mind of James, and they serve little value in this discussion because only God can look into a person's heart and determine whether or not faith exists. All we can do is see the fruit of someone's life.

The person is described as "one of you who should wander (*planao*) from the truth", which carries the meaning of going astray, or apostatizing (Mat 22:29, 24:5, 2 Tim 3:13, Titus 3:3, 2 Pet 2:15). The person in question is not just rejecting the truth of Scripture (the gospel), but is living in a way that stands in stark contrast to the ethical teaching James has detailed in this homily. Believers who accept the truth of God's Word, should live out the truth in their everyday experience! Truth rejected—is truth that is absent from one's everyday lifestyle! The authors of Scripture do not separate truth from lifestyle—they both go hand-in-hand! Therefore, James is envisioning a believer whose ethical conduct has deteriorated along with his belief in the gospel, and he has severed his ties with the community of faith. Spiritually, he's swimming in shark-infested waters!

Someone in the church needs to reach out to him and bring him back! The initiative lies with those in the church to compassionately reach out to the wanderer, do an intervention in the hopes of restoring him back to God, and reestablish him in the community of believers. If someone engages the wanderer in a conversation regarding his spiritual status, the best possible case scenario would be for the wanderer to confess his sins to the brother and receive prayer for restoration (v. 16). This fits neatly into the context of the passage.

James provides incentive to the faithful believers to take the initiative and seek out the wanderer: "remember this: Whoever turns a sinner from the error of their way will save them from death and cover over a multitude of sins (v. 20)." What could be more important than saving someone from death, but in what sense would the sinner be saved from death?

Given the Jewish nature of James' homily, it could be that he is speaking metaphorically about the way of life and the way of death. Walking down the path of sin leads to death, whereas walking down the path of faith and obedience brings life. The evidence of life in a person is the good fruit they bear, just as the evidence of death is the bad fruit one displays. James illustrated this in 1:15 where he said: Then, after desire has conceived, it gives birth to sin; and sin, when it is full-grown, gives birth to death. The point of the illustration being that the way of sin leads to a lifestyle that is characterized by death (rotten fruit).

A second possibility is if the unrepentant sinner continues to walk down the path of sin, God's discipline could come upon the person resulting in sickness or physical death, similar to the situation in 1 Corinthians 11:30. Viewed this way, the one who wanders away from the faith is under God's discipline and dies physically, but his soul goes to heaven. Thus, in this way of viewing the text, James is referring to physical death, when he says "whoever turns a sinner from the error of his way will save him from *physical death.*"

However, physical death doesn't seem to fit the context, so a third possibility is that James is speaking about the worst possible outcome for the unrepentant person—eternal separation from God in hell. Whoever facilitates a sinner's restoration with God alters his eternal destiny from death to life, from hell to heaven!

Additionally, when the sinner turns to God his multitude of sins are covered. Since God forgives the sinner, whatever list of sins that have been compiled are all covered with the blood of Jesus and forgotten (Ps 32:1; Pro 10:12; 1 Pet 4:8). The one doing the restoring can feel good about this, for he has done a great service to the wanderer, and God is glorified! There is a symphony of praise among the angels in heaven when a sinner repents (Luke 15:10).

Those who are used by God to restore the wanderer fulfill four critical tasks: 1. He helps the sinner come to a place of repentance and receive God's forgiveness. 2. Receiving God's forgiveness results in God saving his soul from death. 3. The sinner's long list of sins are covered by God's forgiveness and forgotten. 4. The sinner is restored to fellowship with God's people. These facts should provide incentive to all believers to seek and save the lost as Jesus did (Luke 19:10).

There is evidence in Scripture to suggest that there is spiritual benefit that comes to the one doing the restoring. The Lord told Ezekiel: "But if you do warn the righteous person not to sin and they do not sin, they will surely live because they took warning, and you will have saved yourself (Eze 3:21)." Paul mentioned to Timothy, "Watch your life and doctrine closely. Persevere in them, because if you do, you will save both yourself and your hearers (1 Tim 4:16)."

The conclusion to be drawn from the above passages is that God will treat us as we treat others (Mat 6:14-15, 18:23-35, James 2:12-13). Certainly, if we see a brother wandering from the truth, and we do nothing to warn him, or attempt to bring him back to the path that leads to life, his blood is on our hands (Eze 3:18)!

As James closes his sermon he reminds his readers that spiritual life is serious business! Being right with God brings life, but the path of sin leads to death. Believers need to be living authentic lives for the Lord, and help others who are derailed in their spiritual experience get back on track with God!

Insights and Application, (5:19-20)

One of the harsh realities of being the pastor of a church is that people come and go. Every so often, I think about a person I haven't seen for a while, and I ask the other pastors in our weekly staff meeting if they know anything about that person's whereabouts. The answers that I receive vary from they've been sick, they're traveling, they just moved, they're attending another church, and worst of all they stopped coming to church altogether. In other words, they've become a dropout—they are wandering from the faith!

I'm always sad to hear that someone left my church to attend elsewhere, because it makes me wonder if we were in some way negligent! Did we not care for the person properly, did an incident occur, what happened? Even though it upsets me when someone leaves the church to attend another one, at least they're still attending a church that is faithful to the gospel.

They're still going forward with the Lord, just in a different church. I can live with that!

When someone wanders from the faith, that is an entirely different matter—it is serious stuff! We are responsible to reach out to that person and try to bring them back! God forgive us if we don't! Often times we are aware of a good friend the person has in the church, and we will consult with her about the member who is MIA (missing in action). One of the pastors may call or visit the person to see what's up. The responses vary. They won't take our calls, so we leave a message, a text, but they never respond. There is nothing that we can do to bring the person back to the church if they don't want to talk to us.

All we can do in that case is commend them to God for his care. This is where prayer comes into the picture. James has been talking about how prayer is powerful and effective, and certainly God's people can pray for the wanderer! There have been many times where I've prayed for those who are MIA in staff meetings, in my personal prayer time, in elders meetings, and so forth. Often the only recourse that exists is praying for the one who has wandered from the Lord!

Reading this passage brings a theological issue center stage. Is James saying that you can lose your salvation? This is a hot topic in the body of Christ, resulting in many heated debates among Christians throughout the millennia. There are those that believe that once a person is saved he will always be saved. There are those who believe that in the case of willful deliberate apostasy—which is walking away from Christ—you can lose your salvation. What makes this debate so difficult to resolve is that both positions can be capably defended with Scripture. Space does not permit an exhaustive examination about the accuracy or inaccuracy of either position. That goes beyond the scope of this commentary. The passage under consideration certainly doesn't answer definitively whether or not a believer can lose his salvation!

What is important is that when believers see someone sever their ties with their church, and pursue a lifestyle that deviates from the ethical demands of Scripture, it should grieve our hearts. That person has placed himself in grave spiritual danger! The body of Christ needs to reach out to him and facilitate his restoration. Whether the wanderer is a backslider, nominal believer, seeker who isn't born-again, or whatever other label one places on the individual, the proper response of the faithful Christian is to reach out to the person and do a spiritual intervention!

Sadly, there are those who never return, which is painful and grievous to think about! Perhaps, those who were drifting into the world (4:1-10) and committing spiritual adultery are those James is addressing as wanderers. One wonders what will become of them. James has ended his sermon with an emphasis on prayer, which is powerful and effective! In cases where all attempts to reclaim the dropout have proven to be fruitless, start praying like Elijah, and commend the person to God expecting a miracle.

EPILOGUE

The brand of Christianity that James calls for is the no nonsense type! Reading through the book of James challenges the reader to turn it up a notch for the Lord. If we are going to live for Christ, then let the readers be in the Kingdom with both feet, not being hearers of the word, but doers of the word (1:22). The book of James will be a continual blessing to those in the body of Christ that grapple with its meaning and try to apply it to their lives. I hope this commentary will help you gain insights and understanding into this great book of the Bible.

Blessed is the man who perseveres under trial, because when he has stood the test, he will receive the crown of life that God has promised to those who love him. (James 1:12)

Printed in the United States
By Bookmasters